LGBTQ+ LEADERSHIP IN EDUCATION

This is an essential and timely book that challenges assumptions about who gets to lead and what leadership can look like. Examples of LGBTQ+ leadership span from early years through to higher education, and highlight the power and significance of this work both within formal educational structures and through networks beyond them. This is the book I needed at the start of my career, and the one I will continually return to as a senior leader for guidance, reassurance, and solidarity.

—*Lis Bundock* Associate Dean Education and
Student Experience, School of Education and
the School of Sport and Health Sciences,
University of Brighton

This outstanding book is a necessary and timely contribution to the field of educational leadership offering an honest, personal, and intellectual exploration of LGBTQ+ leadership across the UK education system. Through the voices of sixteen diverse contributors, the book challenges conventional paradigms, examines the role of authenticity, and foregrounds the transformative potential of queer leadership. From early years to higher education, the book weaves together lived experience, critical theory, and policy analysis to highlight the systemic barriers that LGBTQ+ educators can face, as well as the radical hope they can bring in dismantling these obstacles. This title is essential reading for educators, leaders and researchers committed to reimagining what leadership can truly be.

—*Dr Adam Brett* Lecturer and Researcher,
University of Derby, Co-founder of Pride & Progress,
Co-Editor of Critical Insights into LGBTQ+ Inclusive
Education book series

This is a timely and essential book for LGBTQ+ leaders – not only within education but across all sectors. Richly researched yet highly accessible, it amplifies lived experiences that are too often overlooked and underrepresented. At a moment when leadership and inclusion are more critical than ever, this book offers both inspiration and practical insight, leaving readers motivated to drive meaningful and lasting change.

—*Ellis and Lou Beardsmore*, **Co-CEOs Proud Futures.**

Critical Insights into LGBTQ+ Inclusive Education

Series Editors:

Catherine Lee, Anglia Ruskin University, UK
Adam Brett, University of Derby, UK

As researchers, educators and members of the LGBTQ+ community, we are immensely proud to introduce our book series, *Critical Insights into LGBTQ+ Inclusive Education*. This series is both a personal and professional endeavour. Put simply, this collection of books are the titles we wished we could have turned to when we were working as practitioners in schools and universities, and when we began our research careers. In the pages that follow, you will encounter research, experience and innovative thinking that are ambitious, challenging, disruptive and constructive.

The series is borne from the work of our LGBTQ+ Research Network, an active and engaged international collective of over 300 scholars, educators, and practitioners. These are people who come together regularly to share their insights, support one another and ultimately advance LGBTQ+ research. Our contributors come from a broad range of disciplines, career stages and educational settings. Each of these titles showcases the work of those who are committed to creating more inclusive, safe and equitable learning environments for teachers and learners. This series invites action, welcoming diverse voices and perspectives to question convention and spark bold, forward-thinking conversations.

At a time when the rights and protections of LGBTQ+ people are being actively eroded, this book series offers a critically engaged yet resolutely optimistic and solutions-based intervention. The growing prevalence of exclusionary discourse, regressive policy developments and moral panic surrounding sexuality and gender identity underscores the urgent need for this suite of new titles. Each book centres affirmative and forward-looking scholarship that is grounded in the lived realities of LGBTQ+ learners, educators and leaders, many of whom know first-hand what it is to hide who they are.

Each book in the series is designed to explore a specific topic, combining research evidence with practical insight and personal narrative. The scope of the series is deliberately broad. It reflects the complexity of LGBTQ+ inclusion and the many contexts in which it plays out. We also know that LGBTQ+ inclusion does not happen in isolation. It is entwined with other protected characteristics, and this series will highlight the ways in which many minoritised identities intersect and shape experiences in education.

What makes this series distinctive is not only the breadth of its content but the strength of its community. The series emerges from collaborative conversations, mutual encouragement and the sharing of multi-disciplinary expertise that sits at the heart of our LGBTQ+ Research Network. We believe this 'community of practice' approach is itself a challenge to the silos that often dominate academia. This series mirrors the kind of inclusive practice we wish to promote; practice that is relational, practical and grounded in a determination to affect positive change.

This series is also designed to be responsive. Each book is concise enough to provide the agility to react to legislative change, media discourse or shifts in education policy. Our contributors write about issues that are personally significant and often painful, but each also writes about resisting, persisting and creating inclusive spaces of joy, affirmation and new learning.

Each book in this series features one of the 11 colours of the Progress Pride flag on its spine. When placed together, the full collection aims to recreate the flag across your bookshelf. Designed by Daniel Quasar, the Progress Pride flag builds on the traditional rainbow associated with the LGBTQ+ rights movement, adding black and brown stripes to recognise marginalised racialised communities, and pink, blue and white to represent trans identities. We have chosen this design because, like the flag itself, this book series is a compelling representation of our shared histories, collective resilience and ongoing commitment to social justice. At a time when LGBTQ+ inclusion is increasingly contested and under threat, this book series, just like the Progress Pride flag, stands as rallying cry and a call to action. By grounding the series in the visual language of the flag, each book asserts our dedication to intersectionality, visibility, and of course, to progress. It imagines a future where LGBTQ+ inclusion isn't a fight, but a fundamental right; one that is woven into the fabric of every learning space, where inclusion isn't an exception, but an absolute expectation.

FORTHCOMING VOLUME

Queering the Curriculum in Higher Education: Multidisciplinary Perspectives and Best Practices for Transformative Queer Pedagogy

Edited by Sebastian Cordoba

LGBTQ+ LEADERSHIP IN EDUCATION: VISIBILITY, VISION, AND VOICE

EDITED BY

ALEX BAIRD
University of Bedfordshire, UK

CATHERINE LEE
Anglia Ruskin University, UK

CHARLOTTE FEATHER
University of Sunderland, UK

And

DANIEL BURMAN
Anglia Ruskin University, UK

United Kingdom – North America – Japan – India
Malaysia – China

Emerald Publishing Limited
Emerald Publishing, Floor 5, Northspring, 21-23 Wellington Street,
Leeds LS1 4DL

First edition 2026

Editorial matter and selection © 2026 Alex Baird, Catherine Lee,
Charlotte Feather, and Daniel Burman.
Individual chapters © 2026 The authors.
Published under exclusive licence by Emerald Publishing Limited.

Reprints and permissions service
Contact: www.copyright.com

No part of this book may be reproduced, stored in a retrieval system,
transmitted in any form or by any means electronic, mechanical,
photocopying, recording or otherwise without either the prior written
permission of the publisher or a licence permitting restricted copying
issued in the UK by The Copyright Licensing Agency and in the USA by
The Copyright Clearance Center. Any opinions expressed in the chapters
are those of the authors. Whilst Emerald makes every effort to ensure the
quality and accuracy of its content, Emerald makes no representation
implied or otherwise, as to the chapters' suitability and application and
disclaims any warranties, express or implied, to their use.

British Library Cataloguing in Publication Data
A catalogue record for this book is available from the British Library

ISBN: 978-1-80592-616-0 (Print)
ISBN: 978-1-80592-613-9 (Online)
ISBN: 978-1-80592-615-3 (Epub)

INVESTOR IN PEOPLE

CONTENTS

About the Editors   xiii

About the Contributors   xv

1. Introduction   1
   Alex Baird and Charlotte Feather

Section 1: Foundations of LGBTQ+ Leadership: Networks, Early Years and Primary Education

2. Leadership in LGBTQ+ Networks   19
   Jo Brassington

3. Navigating Leadership Without a Map: A Trans Educator's Journey in Early Years   31
   Kelsey-Ann Caldow

4. Navigating Leadership and LGBTQ+ Visibility in Primary Education: Reflections on Section 28, Advocacy and Inclusive Practices   43
   Holly Coull

5. A Quiet Activism: How My Experience as an LGBT+ Teacher and Leader Shapes My Drive for Change in Schools   55
   Gerlinde Achenbach

Section 2: Navigating LGBTQ+ Leadership: Governance, Secondary and Further Education

6. Reflections as a Gay Leader in UK Secondary Schools 69
   Richard McDonald

7. LGBTQ+ Leadership in the Catholic School Context 83
   George White

8. Saying Yes, Saying No: Navigating Being an LGBTQ+ Leader in Secondary Schools and Further Education 97
   Jonny Tridgell

9. Hope Through Supportive and Challenging School Governance 109
   Gary Pykitt

Section 3: Reimagining LGBTQ+ Leadership: Higher Education and Professional Development

10. The Journey of a LGBTQ+ Educator, Researcher and Activist 125
    Alex Baird

11. The Queered Equilibrium: Reframing Leadership and Power for Early-Career Academics 137
    Charlotte Feather

12. Empowering LGBTQ+ Leaders in Higher Education: Navigating Identity, Inclusion and Career Progression 157
    Catherine Lee and Daniel Burman

13. Teaching the Future Leaders: Learning and Training to Become a Successful LGBTQ+ Leader Within Higher Education   173
Helen Bushell-Thornalley

Section 4: Transforming LGBTQ+ Leadership: Systems, Structures and Community

14. Follow the Leader? Critically Questioning LGBT+ Leadership in the Surveillance University   185
Pippa Sterk

15. Lessons Learnt Becoming UCL IOE's First and Only   195
Simon Liu

16. Leaving to Lead: Reimagining Inclusion in Higher Education as a Black, Neurodivergent, Lesbian Leader   209
Catherine Millan

17. Conclusion   221
Catherine Lee and Daniel Burman

ABOUT THE EDITORS

Dr Alex Baird (They/Them) is a Senior Lecturer in Sport and Physical Education at the University of Bedfordshire. They serve as the co-chair of the LGBTQ+ Alliance Staff Network and have played a significant role in leading Diversity, Equality, and Inclusion (DEI) initiatives across the university. Their EdD thesis research focused on a unique LGBTQ+ Leadership Development programme at a UK university, which was founded and led by Professor Catherine Lee MBE, and co-led by Dan Burman. Before their work in higher education, Alex taught for 12 years in both primary and secondary education.

Professor Catherine Lee MBE (She/Her) is the Pro Vice-Chancellor and the Dean at Anglia Ruskin University. Her research focuses on LGBTQ+ inclusion, teacher education and educational leadership. Catherine's experiences as a teacher during Section 28 inspired the BAFTA nominated feature film *Blue Jean* and in 2023, she was awarded an MBE for services to Equality in Education.

Charlotte Feather (She/Her) is an early-career academic recently promoted to Senior Lecturer at the University of Sunderland, where she leads the Masters in Special Educational Needs, Disability and Inclusion. Her specialisms include LGBTQ+ inclusive education, professional identity development and critical pedagogies for social justice. Charlotte co-chairs the university's Staff Pride Network and leads on DEI training both institutionally and with external partners. She is also the creator of the LGBTQ+ Primary Hub, which supports primary practitioners in creating more inclusive educational spaces.

Daniel Burman (He/Him) is a Senior Business Operations Manager for the Faculty of Science and Engineering at Anglia Ruskin University. With a dedicated focus on LGBTQ+ leadership and the civic responsibilities of organisations. Dan's research aims to foster inclusive and equitable environments. He co-leads both the LGBTQ+ and Men's Staff Networks at ARU, championing initiatives that promote equity, diversity and inclusion. Dan is a passionate advocate for creating spaces where everyone can thrive.

ABOUT THE CONTRIBUTORS

Gerlinde Achenbach FCCT (She/Her) is an education consultant and executive coach working in LGBT+ inclusion and school improvement. Gerlinde's career in schools and the wider education sector spans over 35 years. A former primary Headteacher, Gerlinde's schools were recognised both nationally and internationally for high quality, inclusive practice and provision.

Jo Brassington (They/Them) is an educator and a trainer whose work creates more inclusive educational spaces. Jo is the co-founder of Pride & Progress, and their award-winning book 'Pride & Progress: Making Schools LGBT+ Inclusive Spaces' has changed practice and improved schools for LGBT+ teachers and students. At the time of writing, Jo is in the first year of a PhD, researching LGBT+ networks in education.

Dr Helen Bushell-Thornalley (She/Her) is a Senior Lecturer in Secondary ITE Physical Education and Dance at Lincoln Bishop University, Lincoln, and a founding member of the Base for Research, Inclusion, Diversity and Equality (BRIDgE) across the university. Prior to her work in Higher Education, Dr Helen taught for 13 years within London Secondary schools where she held academic, curriculum and pastoral leadership roles. Helen also performed at an elite level within sports teams that were recognised and honoured at national and international levels.

Kelsey-Ann Caldow (They/Them) has worked in education for over 15 years, from early years to youth work, within formal and non-formal education settings, working with children and young people across diverse social and cultural contexts. As a trans, non-binary and queer educator, Kelsey-Ann brings a lived commitment to equity and inclusion, using their platform to challenge structural barriers and cultivate belonging from the earliest stages of education. Their research informs their holistic approach to inclusive practice, particularly within Early Years. Kelsey-Ann regularly speaks at national and international conferences to promote good practice and has delivered LGBTIQ+ inclusion training across Scotland and Europe.

Holly Coull (She/Her) is the Teaching and Learning Lead at Rise Multi-Academy Trust. Prior to this role, she was a headteacher and spent 15 years teaching in primary schools. Holly founded 'Pride at Rise', which includes an LGBTQ+ staff network and newsletter. Her work in this area has expanded into broader efforts around Diversity, Equality, and Inclusion (DEI), and she is now a member of Rise's DEI working group.

Simon Liu (He/Him) is the first and only to date Faculty LGBTQ+ Equity Lead for the Institute of Education (IOE, UCL's Faculty of Education and Society). He has spearheaded the faculty's development of awareness, inclusion and advocacy for its LGBTQ+ staff and students. Previously, he was the LGBTQ+ Intersectional Lead for the faculty's successful Athena SWAN Silver Award application. He is also a member of the university-wide LGBTQ+ Equality Steering Group (LESG), which is regularly consulted by the university as well as promotes LGBTQ+ representation. As his main job, he is a teacher of English for Academic Purposes preparing students for, mainly, postgraduate entry at UCL.

Richard McDonald (He/Him) is an Assistant Principal across a MAT in Yorkshire. Richard began his teaching career as a Teacher of English, undertaking both subject and senior leadership roles in different schools in the area before appointment to his current post. While studying for a MBA in Educational Leadership, Richard completed a dissertation exploring the experiences and impact of LGBT+ leaders in UK secondary schools. He is now looking forward to developing this further by undertaking a PhD on the representation of LGBT+ leaders in UK schools.

Catherine Millan (She/Her) is an award-winning equity and inclusion specialist, founder of Be What You See Consultancy and a recognised leader in challenging systemic discrimination in Education and the workplace. With over a decade of experience in the Education and charitable sectors, including international humanitarian work, she specialises in designing transformative training that empowers organisations to create psychologically safe, inclusive environments. A proud Black, neurodivergent lesbian, her work is rooted in lived experience and driven by purpose, focusing on creating long-term, structural change through education and community engagement.

Gary Pykitt (He/Him) is a Senior Lecturer in Primary Education at Birmingham City University and the Chair of Governors for a small federation of primary schools in Derbyshire. He is currently working towards his Professional Doctorate in Education with a working title, '*A hopeful future? A critical exploration of the possibilities for teachers enabling LGBT+ representation and inclusivity in mainstream primary schools.*'

Dr Pippa Sterk (Any Pronouns) is a Postdoctoral Teaching Fellow in Education, at King's College London. Dr Pippa work focuses on community-focused, creative pedagogical practice and using education for social justice. Outside their academic work, they are a creative writer and cultural producer.

Jonny Tridgell (He/Him) has taught in secondary and further education since 2009. He has held multiple roles, including Assistant Headteacher, Head of Sixth Form, Head of Department and Lead Practitioner. Other roles have included being a university diversity officer and a lead examiner in religious studies. He currently works in teacher education and educational research in the University of Oxford, where he is also Chair of the LGBT+ Staff Network and a DPhil student.

George White (He/Him) is a transgender man and a Catholic teacher of Religious Education at the Catholic school he attended as a child and was baptised in at the age of 16. He holds a BA in Philosophy and Theology from Heythrop College, an MA in Global Ethics and Human Values from King's College London and a Secondary PGCE in Religious Studies from the University of Cambridge.

1

INTRODUCTION

ALEX BAIRD[a] AND CHARLOTTE FEATHER[b]

[a]University of Bedfordshire, UK
[b]University of Sunderland, UK

BEGINNINGS

This book began with a conversation. While we come from different professional backgrounds and are at varying stages of our careers, the four editors were united by a shared recognition: that LGBTQ+ leadership in education remains underexplored, underacknowledged and too often underestimated—even by those enacting it. What started as a reflective dialogue about our own experiences and research findings quickly evolved into a wider commitment to amplify the voices of LGBTQ+ educators who are leading across the United Kingdom's early years, primary, secondary and tertiary sectors. We are delighted that this book forms part of the *Critical Insights into LGBTQ+ Inclusive Education* Book Series.

Until now, literature on LGBTQ+ leadership has been predominantly rooted in the United States and framed through the lens of corporate business contexts. As a result, the distinct values and challenges, and cultural nuances of

LGBTQ+ leadership within UK education have been largely overlooked. With this in mind, we set out to create a space in which queer educational leadership could be both visible and valued. Here, leadership is not explored as a fixed role or title, but as a set of everyday practices and ways of being.

Sixteen diverse voices from the LGBTQ+ community are represented in this book. Each contributor offers a unique perspective, shaped by their own positionality, career stage and educational setting. Our hope is that this collection will encourage readers, whether LGBTQ+ leaders or allies, to revisit the concept of leadership and find affirmation, challenge or inspiration in these pages.

We are incredibly grateful to all our contributors for the care and commitment they have shown in helping to bring this book to life. Their chapters speak to the transformative power of education, for themselves and their learners, and to the complex responsibilities that come with leading as LGBTQ+ individuals. While their stories are distinct, common threads run throughout: the enduring legacy of Section 28 (LGA, 1988), the ongoing negotiation of identity, the tension between visibility and vulnerability and a critical questioning of what leadership is – and what it could be.

This book invites readers to challenge conventional understandings of leadership, and we hope that the honesty and bravery of its contributors prompt reflection on your own role in shaping more inclusive educational spaces.

LANGUAGE AND IDENTITY

While we generally use the term LGBTQ+ throughout this book as an inclusive umbrella term, we recognise its limitations and complexities. In this context, the initials stand for

Lesbian, Gay, Bisexual, Trans, Queer, with the plus sign (+) denoting other sexual and gender minorities whose identities fall outside cisgender and heterosexual norms. At times, we have mirrored the terminology used in relevant policy or guidance documents, and contributors were encouraged to use the language and initialism that best reflects their own identity.

Some contributors use the reclaimed term 'queer', a word that has become a powerful tool of self-definition and political resistance for many. However, we acknowledge and appreciate that for some within the LGBTQ+ community, this term still carries the weight of historical violence and may be experienced as a slur. We hold space for both its affirming and painful connotations.

Throughout this book, the concept of intersectionality—a concept first coined by Kimberlé Crenshaw in 1989—offers a critical lens for understanding the layered and interwoven nature of identity. Intersectionality considers how different dimensions of identity such as gender, sexuality, race, class, disability and more overlap to shape individual experiences and the complexities of power. Contributors reflect on how their multiple identities and experiences have affected the various stages of their leadership journeys and influenced the qualities they bring to leadership. In doing so, this book recognises and contextualises the diverse experiences of LGBTQ+ educators within the UK education system.

The theme of 'coming out' also features across several chapters. It is understood not as a singular moment but as an ongoing, multifaceted and often transformative process for many LGBTQ+ people. The meaning of coming out varies for everyone and may shift from affirmation of a non-heterosexual sexuality and/or non-cisgender identity to oneself, to disclosing to friends and family, or to not disclosing at all. While visibility and representation can be powerful tools against silence and shame, we are also mindful that remaining silent is not synonymous with failure, fear or a lack of integrity. Reasons for not putting one's head above the parapet, given the risks attached, real or assumed, particularly in a work setting are understandable. We recognise that this book is written by LGBTQ+ educators who have chosen to be out in their professional contexts. As such, it may not capture the experiences of those who remain closeted at work. Their stories, though absent from these pages, are no less valid or important. Silence, too, can be a strategy of resilience.

AUTHENTICITY AND LEADERSHIP

Many of the authors reflect on the concept of 'authenticity', highlighting that it involves far more than simply coming out—or feeling pressured to do so. Authenticity, in this context, is not a one-time act of disclosure but an ongoing process of personal reflexivity to develop a strong, affirming sense of self and self-awareness. Authentic leadership, then, is not about meeting a checklist of identity markers. It requires the integration of an evolving self into one's professional ethos—navigating how personal values and identity shape decision-making, relationships, and leadership style. For LGBTQ+ educators, this process can be both empowering and fraught, especially when authenticity risks marginalisation or harm.

Despite these complexities, there remains a distinct lack of leadership development resources tailored specifically to the needs and realities of LGBTQ+ educators. LGBTQ+ leadership development programmes, as explored in Chapters 10 and 12, provide vital spaces for leaders to come together to share their personal and professional narratives, explore the interplay between identity and leadership and reimagine leadership practices that are rooted in integrity and community.

POWER AND POSSIBILITY

Leadership theory is, and always has been, a contested terrain. Early theories tended to take an individualistic perspective by focusing on the characteristics of successful leaders, which often upheld hierarchical and masculinised ideals of authority. Later approaches expanded to include the role of followers and the influence of broader situational circumstances. Yet, despite these developments, many mainstream theories still underestimate how leadership is shaped by power relations, and how those power relations are unequally distributed.

The contributors to this book interrogate the intricacies of power dynamics that have often been left underexplored, such as informal leadership and the resistance of followers. Traditional views of leadership remain constrained by individualistic, fixed and binary categorisations: leader versus follower, male versus female, powerful versus powerless. These binaries not only obscure the realities of leadership in practice but also reinforce existing inequalities and exclude those whose leadership does not conform.

Many of the authors in this book highlight the vulnerabilities and tensions they encounter in leadership roles within heteronormative environments, where their leadership is often unrecognised or devalued. They also challenge and resist the dominant norms surrounding the concept of leadership to propose an alternative understanding. This alternative vision embraces vulnerability as strength, and sees leadership not as control or charisma but as a commitment to equity, creativity and community. The work of leading LGBTQ+ networks, driving Diversity, Equality and Inclusion (DEI) initiatives and fostering inclusive cultures becomes a powerful act of leadership – one that challenges the status quo and offers resilient, imaginative responses to the systemic inequities within education.

CONTEXT AND CLIMATE

Legislative progress in the United Kingdom, such as the Equality Act, 2010, The Marriage (Same Sex Couples) Act, 2013 and the Sexual Harassment Duty, 2024, has contributed to the removal of some structural barriers to LGBTQ+ inclusion and leadership. These legal shifts, alongside growing social acceptance, have helped create more supportive environments for LGBTQ+ employees across sectors, including education. However, significant challenges persist (McCay, 2024; Ebrey & Haworth, 2025) and hostility towards LGBTQ+ individuals is on the rise due to heightened negative political and media attention (Wyatt, 2025).

Globally, there have been some important gains: marriage equality has been introduced in Greece and Thailand; same-sex relations have been decriminalised in Namibia and Dominica; and new self-identification laws have been implemented in Germany, Ecuador and Puerto Rico. Yet these advancements are paralleled by a surge in anti-LGBTQ+ legislation in countries such as Ghana, Iraq, Mali, Georgia, Bulgaria, Liberia, Burkina Faso, Trinidad and Tobago, Poland, the Czech Republic, Hungary and Russia. These laws often target gender-diverse individuals and reinforce nationalistic and heteronormative ideals, placing LGBTQ+ people at heightened risk. In the United States, the Trump administration has actively rolled back LGBTQ+ rights, issuing executive orders that restrict protections in education, healthcare and the workplace. Of particular concern is the dismantling of DEI initiatives—an ideological stance that is gaining traction across right-wing political movements globally. These developments may have a chilling effect beyond the United States, including UK institutions, where DEI policies and LGBTQ+ inclusion efforts increasingly find themselves under scrutiny.

At the time of writing, the United Kingdom has fallen to its lowest ever position of 22nd out of 49 European countries ranked for LGBTI-inclusive political and legal practices, making it now the lowest-ranked country in Western Europe for LGBTI rights (ILGA-Europe, 2025). Ten years ago, the United Kingdom was ranked first (ILGA-Europe, 2015). When focusing specifically on trans rights, the United Kingdom currently ranks 45th of 49. This sharp decline reflects growing concern from international and domestic bodies alike. Recent legal and political developments have been key contributors to this regression. The 2025 ruling by the Supreme Court that the word 'sex' in the Equality Act, 2010 was used to refer to biological sex rather than legal gender acquired through a Gender Recognition Certificate (GRC), alongside now retracted guidance issued by the Equality and Human Rights Commission (2025), has significantly undermined the rights and protections of trans individuals. While the full implications of the ruling are not yet clear, there is growing concern that it will further restrict access and protections for transgender people, thereby legitimising exclusionary practices and contributing to a climate of increased hostility and marginalisation.

Despite longstanding calls for reform, the UK government has yet to introduce a ban on conversion therapy that includes protections for trans people, leaving many vulnerable to coercive and damaging practices. In the workplace, there has been a decline in DEI initiatives due in part to the challenging economic climate but also reflective of a broader cultural and political backlash against inclusion work. These shifts in cultural and legislative climate are mirrored, and often intensified, within education policy itself, as explored in the next section.

POLICY AND REGULATION

In the school sector, recent policy developments have raised serious concerns about the erosion of LGBTQ+ inclusion. The *Relationships Education, Relationships and Sex Education, and Health Education (RSHE) Draft Guidance* (DfE, 2023) proposes restrictions on the inclusion of LGBTQ+ themes, potentially kerbing young people's access to accurate and affirming information. In parallel, the *Gender Questioning Children: Non-Statutory Guidance for Schools and Colleges* (DfE, 2024) draft for consultation – which the Minister for Education in Jersey recently stated would not be revoked—has been widely criticised for its failure to uphold the rights and dignity of trans and non-binary pupils. These developments are further compounded by the *Cass Review* (2024), which, despite its stated concern for safeguarding, has contributed to a highly polarised and politicised discourse around gender identity in education.

In higher education, similar tensions are unfolding. The decision by several UK universities to disassociate from Stonewall's *Workplace Equality Index*—a benchmarking tool for LGBTQ+ inclusion – raises concerns, particularly given the growing influence of gender critical perspectives within the sector. While the *Higher Education (Freedom of Speech) Act* (2023) and its proposed changes (DfE, 2025) seek to protect against censorship and promote open expression, its emphasis on debate over dialogue risks reinforcing power imbalances. In practice, this may enable dominant voices to frame gender identity as a topic for public contestation, potentially creating unsafe or exclusionary environments for trans and non-binary people. Moreover, the Office for Students (2025) has now issued guidance encouraging universities to revise their DEI policies, following its decision to fine an English university in a high-profile case. Together, these developments suggest a shifting regulatory climate in which the principles of inclusion and belonging are increasingly subordinated to narrative of neutrality, debate and institutional compliance.

REIMAGINING LEADERSHIP

The UK educational landscape is currently marked by a series of significant challenges which include chronic underfunding, widespread industrial action in response to redundancies and pay disputes, shifting regulatory demands, rapid technological change and entrenched inequalities. In this complex and often volatile environment, the importance of inclusive, values-led leadership has never been more urgent. Beyond simply increasing the number of visible LGBTQ+ leaders, we recognise the distinct and critical vantage point that LGBTQ+ leaders offer to disrupt conventional notions of 'straight' leadership and challenge the prevailing cisnormative and heteronormative conventions of UK education sectors.

Crucially, we reject the notion that transformation should fall on the shoulders of individuals alone. Instead, this book unites a collective of voices to harness our radical potential. Through these interwoven narratives, we offer not just critique but hope. By centring *visibility*, offering bold *vision* and raising our collective *voice*, this book seeks to que(e)ry the very foundations of leadership in education. The chapters that follow bring together a rich tapestry of voices, each one offering a unique perspective on what it means to lead as an LGBTQ+ educator in the UK today.

OVERVIEW OF CHAPTERS

Section 1 – Foundations of LGBTQ+ Leadership: Networks, Early Years and Primary Education

In Chapter 2, Jo Brassington begins by describing how their personal desire for an LGBTQ+ network, what they describe as part of their 'regayssance', led to the co-creation of *Pride and Progress*. They reflect on the power of LGBTQ+ networks to foster leadership beyond formal roles, highlighting the benefits for individuals, communities and organisations alike. Chapter 3 turns to the early years sector, where Kelsey-Ann Caldow considers how LGBTQ+ leadership and DEI initiatives, when supported by senior leadership, can contribute to safer, more joyful childhood experiences. In Chapter 4, Holly Coull, a former primary headteacher now working as a teaching and learning lead within a multi-academy trust, shares her reflections on the legacy of Section 28 and the tensions of working within a faith school. Holly emphasises the transformative impact of visible role models and supportive allies in enabling her to introduce LGBTQ+ inclusive initiatives, such as themed books, Pride events and staff networks—resources that were notably absent during her own schooling. Bridging the primary and secondary sectors, Chapter 5 is written by Gerlinde Achenbach, a former headteacher who now works as an education consultant. Gerlinde reflects on her quiet activism and the ways in which her lived experiences have shaped her leadership values. She also offers advice to emerging LGBTQ+ educators, navigating leadership in a moment shaped by both progress and backlash.

Section 2 – Navigating LGBTQ+ Leadership: Governance, Secondary and Further Education

Richard McDonald begins the secondary school section in Chapter 6 by exploring the intersections of overlapping identities, drawing on his own work and leadership. He, like Holly in Chapter 4, underscores the pivotal role of allyship in enabling inclusive leadership and creating supportive educational environments. In Chapter 7, George White examines LGBTQ+ leadership within Catholic education, offering a clear framework of how LGBTQ+ inclusive leadership and initiatives might exist in alignment with UK law. His chapter provides valuable insights for educators navigating faith-based settings where tensions around inclusion may be particularly pronounced. Chapter 8, written by Jonny Tridgell, explores the complexities of navigating LGBTQ+ identities in both secondary schools and further education settings. Jonny offers a candid reflection on the questions he faced and how he navigated both the benefits and challenges of offering visible LGBTQ+ leadership. This section concludes with Chapter 9, in which Gary Pykitt focuses on the vital role of inclusive and critically conscious school governance. Drawing on his experience as an educator and governor, he argues that meaningful and sustainable change in schools depends on leadership at all levels that is informed by equity and critical reflection.

Section 3 – Reimagining LGBTQ+ Leadership: Higher Education and Professional Development

Section 3 opens with Alex Baird in Chapter 10, who reflects on their transition from working in schools to a role in higher education. Alex shares how they navigated this shift and ultimately found ways to align their teaching, research and DEI work, offering insight into the evolving nature of LGBTQ+ leadership across contexts. In Chapter 11, Charlotte Feather critically examines dominant leadership paradigms through the lens of LGBTQ+ early-career academics in higher education. Drawing on lived experiences and broader reflections, this chapter explores the complexities of identity, visibility and leadership—raising themes that will resonate with early-career leaders across a variety of educational contexts. Chapter 12 delves into the rationale, composition and outcomes of a pioneering LGBTQ+ leadership development programme in UK higher education. This chapter highlights the value of intentional spaces for leadership growth, connection and professional development. In Chapter 13, Helen Bushell-Thornalley reflects on her academic leadership within the disciplines of Teacher Education, Physical Education, Sport, and Dance (PESSD). Helen explores the possibilities of shifting institutional cultures from within and inspiring the next generation of teachers.

Section 4 – Transforming LGBTQ+ Leadership: Systems, Structures and Community

Section 4 expands the conversation, turning a critical lens towards the broader structures within which LGBTQ+ leadership operates. In Chapter 14, Pippa Sterk interrogates the relationship between leaders, institutions and the communities they serve. The chapter challenges readers to consider how leadership can reproduce, as well as resist, institutional norms, and ends with a powerful call for leaders to consider what we might be complicit in through our practices. In Chapter 15, Simon Liu draws from his extensive experience in DEI to explore the systemic nature of inequality within educational institutions. He emphasises the importance of understanding organisational structure, identifying inequalities, facilitating conversations with diverse perspectives and ultimately fostering positive changes in workplace cultures. Before our concluding reflections, Chapter 16 sees Catherine Millan reflect on her leadership across education and community spaces. Her chapter offers an affirming and empowering message that encourages readers to embrace leadership as both a personal and collective endeavour.

A FINAL WORD

Together, these chapters offer insight, provocation and hope. They invite us to consider how leadership can be redefined through the lens of lived experience, critical reflection and collective action. As you move through the chapters that follow, we encourage you to read with openness to the challenges shared, the strategies offered and the possibilities imagined for a more inclusive and just educational landscape. We hope you find connection, guidance and space for reflection—and that this book offers both affirmation and inspiration, wherever you are on your leadership journey.

REFERENCES

Cass, H. (2024). *Independent review of gender identity services for children and young people: Final report.* NHS.

Crenshaw, K. (1989). Demarginalizing the intersection of race and sex: A black feminist critique of antidiscrimination doctrine, feminist theory and antiracist politics. *University of Chicago Legal Forum, 1989*(1), 139–167.

Department for Education. (2023). *Gender questioning children: Non-statutory guidance for schools and colleges (draft for consultation).* Available at: https://consult.education.gov.uk/equalities-political-impartiality-anti-bullying-team/gender-questioning-children-proposed-guidance/supporting_documents/Gender%20Questioning%20Children%20%20nonstatutory%20guidance.pdf

Department for Education. (2024). *Relationships, sex and health education: Draft guidance for consultation.* Available at: Relationships Education, Relationships and Sex Education and Health Education guidance

Department for Education. (2025). *The future of the higher education (Freedom of Speech) act* (2023). Available at: The future of the Higher Education (Freedom of Speech) Act 2023 - GOV.UK

Ebrey, J., & Haworth, R. (2025). *The Pride in leadership report. Barriers to LGBTQ+ career development in the UK.* Available at: https://prideinleadership.co.uk/LGBTQ-career-barriers-report-2025

Equality Act. (2010). c. 15. Available at: *Equality Act, 2010*

Equality and Human Rights Commission. (2025, April 25). *An interim update on the practical implications of the UK Supreme Court judgment.* Available at: An interim update on the practical implications of the UK Supreme Court judgment | EHRC

ILGA-Europe. (2015). *Annual review of the human rights situation of lesbian, gay, bisexual, trans, and intersex people in Europe.* Available at: Annual Review 2015 | ILGA-Europe

ILGA-Europe. (2025). *Trans rights and wellbeing in Europe and Central Asia: Annual review.* Available at: Trans Rights Index & Map 2025: The new trans tipping point and Europe's struggle for self-determination - TGEU - Trans Europe and Central AsiaTGEU – Trans Europe and Central Asia

Local Government Act.(1988). *Section 28.* Available online: www.legislation.gov.uk/ukpga/1988/9/contents (accessed on 13 2021, December).

Marriage (Same Sex Couples) Act. (2013). *c. 30.* Available at: https://assets.publishing.service.gov.uk/media/5a750cd2e5274a59fa717007/140423_M_SSC_Act_factsheet__web_version_.pdf

McCay, L. (2024). *Breaking the rainbow ceiling: How LGBTQ+ people can thrive and succeed at work.* Bloomsbury Business.

Office for Students. (2025). *University of Sussex fined £585,000 for free speech and governance breaches.* Available at https://www.officeforstudents.org.uk/publications/regulatory-case-report-for-university-of-sussex/

Sexual Harassment Duty. (2024). In *Equality Act 2010 (amendment)*. Available at: New protections from sexual harassment come into force - GOV.UK

Wyatt, H. (2025). 'We're all ready to fight back and stand together': 7 LGBTQIA+ people on how Pride feels different this year. *Cosmopolitan*. Available at: Pride 2025: LGBTQ people on how Pride feels different this year

Section 1

FOUNDATIONS OF LGBTQ+ LEADERSHIP: NETWORKS, EARLY YEARS AND PRIMARY EDUCATION

2

LEADERSHIP IN LGBTQ+ NETWORKS

JO BRASSINGTON

Pride & Progress, UK

Keywords: LGBTQ+ networks; theoretical framework for diverse networks; LGBTQ+ leadership; LGBTQ+ leadership development; effective school leadership skills

A DESIRE FOR CONNECTION

My finger hesitated over the button for some time before eventually hitting 'Send Tweet'.

It was still called Twitter in those days, and I predict I will always stubbornly refuse to call it by any other name. I had typed the tweet without much thought but had since spent an unreasonable amount of time building up the courage to share it. After tapping send, I refreshed the page and waited in anticipation. As I nervously stared at my phone screen, there was no way I could have known that this moment would shape my career in education and go on to teach me so much about LGBTQ+ leadership.

Six months prior to posting the tweet, I had, for the first time, met an LGBTQ+ teacher who was open about being gay in their school. I was a few years into my career when we met, and until our conversation, I had never considered the possibility that a teacher could be openly LGBTQ+ in their classroom. I, like many others, was educated under the shadow that Section 28 cast on our educational spaces (Baker, 2022; Lee, 2023), so when I later re-entered these spaces as a teacher, I carried with me the silence and shame it created.

My first conversation with an out LGBTQ+ teacher was brief, but it empowered me to come out in my own school the following week in response to homophobic language being used in my classroom. Coming out in an educational space for the first time was frightening, but it was also liberating beyond words. I was no longer hiding, pretending to be somebody else, and treading lightly for fear of being caught out. It felt like fully arriving in my classroom for the first time.

The knowledge that other LGBTQ+ teachers existed, paired with the liberation of having come out myself, changed my paradigm (a period of my life which I once referred to as 'my regayssance', much to my friends' disapproval). I was desperate to connect with other LGBTQ+ educators, to share experiences and find community.

Not long after my desire for network and community had been ignited, it was stopped in its tracks by the announcement of the first COVID-19 lockdown in March 2020. Months of lockdown passed, and my desire for community grew stronger – an experience shared by many LGBTQ+ people (LGBT Foundation, 2023). Until, on the 1 June 2020, when I nervously hit send on that tweet.

Leadership in LGBTQ+ Networks

> Pride Month is usually a time where our community comes together, and this year I am disappointed to be missing out on that support. Would any teachers be interested if I organised an event online for LGBTQ+ educators to get together, share experiences, celebrate pride and begin to build a support network for those who need it?
> @jobrassington 01/06/2020.

I was surprised by the scale of the positive response, and a few weeks later, the online LGBTQ+ educator's pride was enough of a success for me to immediately start planning our next event. Through the remainder of 2020, I found myself running a series of online LGBTQ+ network events, which is how I got to know Dr Adam Brett. Off the back of these events, and Adam's doctoral research, we co-founded *Pride & Progress*: a podcast, platform and community network which works to amplify the voices of LGBTQ+ educators and create more inclusive educational spaces. Suddenly, and accidently, I had found myself co-leading an LGBTQ+ network.

At the time of writing, Adam and I have been running Pride & Progress together for over four years. During that time, I have also held various positions of middle-leadership in schools including subject leadership, key stage leadership, curriculum leadership and for a while acting assistant headteacher. While each of these roles granted me leadership lessons, it has been my work with Pride & Progress that has taught me the most about leadership and helped me to develop my skills as an LGBTQ+ leader. If I were to enter a middle or senior leadership position in education again, I would be more confident and competent as a result of the professional development that leadership with an LGBTQ+ network has provided me.

Most LGBTQ+ networks, like Pride & Progress, start from a desire for connection or social support and develop organically from that starting point (Raeburn, 2004). For this reason, such networks are not often associated with leadership development, but I believe they should be. In this chapter, I am going to suggest that involvement in an LGBTQ+ network is a valuable opportunity to empower and develop leadership. Whatever your leadership experience level, there is much to be learned through intentional engagement with LGBTQ+ networks.

DEFINING LGBTQ+ NETWORKS

I imagine humans have always formed networks informed by identity, but the concept of identity-based employee networks emerges as affinity groups based on ethnicity, in response to racism in North America during the 1960s (Douglas, 2008). Other identity networks followed, and the history of LGBTQ+ employee networks specifically can be traced for over 50 years under various names such as: employee networks, affinity groups or identity networks (Githens & Aragon, 2009). Such networks began in low numbers in the 1970s, which marginally increased during the 1980s, and became substantially more common in the 1990s (Githens & Aragon, 2009; Raeburn, 2004). In the United Kingdom specifically, these networks have often had an entangled relationship with trade unions (Colgan et al., 2012).

Despite a history of over 50 years, there remains a 'dearth of research on LGBT+ networks in academic literature' (McFadden & Crowley-Henry, 2018, p. 1057). In fact, I am still unable to find a single study, which explores LGBTQ+ employee networks specifically in the context of educational spaces (this is part of the rationale for my current PhD research). One challenge in this new research area is that scholars have yet to agree on a shared definition of employee networks. It is surprisingly common for researchers to offer no definition at all.

However, several defining features emerge from those who have offered definitions. Most obviously, the members of the network must 'share a common identity' (Beavers, 2023, p. 1420) and come 'from traditionally disadvantaged or minority demographics' (CIPD, 2021, p. 2). In this context, members of the network will all identify as LGBTQ+ (although some allies may be involved). Furthermore, Parales (2002) defines networks as 'formal or semi-formal internal groups of employees established to create a respectful and inclusive workplace culture' (p. 2). The emphasis on formal or semi-formal distinguishes LGBTQ+ networks from informal social connections. If two lesbian colleagues talk in the staffroom, this may be meaningful social connection, but it would not constitute an LGBTQ+ employee network in the way the literature conceptualises them. Pareles' definition also emphasises the internal nature of the group. Given the interconnected nature of workplace networks and trade union networks in the United Kingdom (Colgan & McKearney, 2012; Colgan et al., 2012), and the now common school structure of Multi-Academy Trusts (MATs), it would be appropriate to understand internal in this context as meaning within the same workplace, the same union or the same profession. In addition, and crucially for their success, such networks should be in some way 'seeking to improve the workplace environment' (Githens & Aragon, 2009, p. 133). With these nuances in mind, this chapter defines LGBTQ+

employee networks as: a group of LGBTQ+ employees who work in the same workplace or profession coming together formally or semi-formally to work towards improving their workplace or profession for LGBTQ+ people.

Of course, networks (even under this definition) vary in size, in goals and in how they are organised (Githens & Aragon, 2009). In education, there are arguably three different models. Firstly, there are the institution level LGBTQ+ networks, such as networks in specific schools, MATs, colleges or universities. These networks are often small and work on promoting LGBTQ+ inclusion within that specific institution. Secondly, there are the trade union level LGBTQ+ networks. For example, the National Education Union has LGBTQ+ networks that operate both nationally and regionally, as well as specific intersectional and identity networks. These are part of a larger trade union, and they work to promote LGBTQ+ inclusion within their union and the wider profession. Thirdly, there are what I have come to refer to as community LGBTQ+ networks. These are networks that exist outside of specific institutions and unions, such as our network Pride & Progress. They connect individuals beyond the bounds of specific workplaces or trade union membership and might therefore work towards broader goals of inclusion within the profession or professional community.

Whatever the model of LGBTQ+ network, there is an increasing volume of evidence (albeit currently outside of the specific context of educational spaces) which demonstrates the value of involvement with them. Research highlights that involvement in LGBTQ+ networks can offer social support; remedy feelings of isolation; act as a mechanism for employee voice and improve the wider workplace (Colgan et al., 2006; Colgan & McKearney, 2010; Githens & Aragon, 2009;

McFadden & Crowley-Henry, 2018; McFadden et al., 2024). In their review of literature regarding diversity networks, Dennissen et al. (2019) observe that there is a lack of theoretical frameworks which capture this potential. They go on to suggest a three-level framework:

- Level 1, Individual Level: Career Development.
- Level 2, Group Level: Community Building.
- Level 3, Organisational Level: Inclusion.

This framework is a useful way to help visualise the widening concentric circles of potential that LGBTQ+ networks hold. However, the first level is often overlooked. As we have identified, people start or join LGBTQ+ networks because they recognise the group level potential. As in my story which opened this chapter, an LGBTQ+ educator seeks community and therefore engages with an existing network or creates their own. These networks often develop organically, during which the focus may broaden to consider the organisational level potential of inclusion (Raeburn, 2004). However, the individual level potential in relation to career development, and within that leadership development, can thus be overlooked.

HOW LGBTQ+ NETWORKS DEVELOP LEADERSHIP

After reviewing the major literature on school leadership, Leithwood et al. (2008) conclude that the same leadership practices make up the repertoire of almost all successful leaders. The review, updated in 2020 (Leithwood et al., 2020), identifies four key domains of practice, including: setting direction, building relationships and developing people, developing the organisational to support desired practices and improving the instructional programme.

The skills required within each of these domains of practice could, of course, be developed through traditional middle and senior leadership positions. However, some scholars have begun to explore how networks could also be powerful in developing these practices (Leithwood & Azah, 2016), and I can think of countless examples of how I personally, and other colleagues involved in LGBTQ+ networks, have utilised and developed these same leadership domains in our work in networks. An LGBTQ+ network not only has to set the direction of the network, but they can also go on to lead the direction of the organisation more broadly through their work (Raeburn, 2004). They may build a shared vision, identify goals and communicate these both within their group and beyond. A key part of this communication is the building of relationships. For an LGBTQ+ network to have broader impact, they must learn to communicate beyond their network members, often by leading the delivery of training, leading the distribution of key information and considering ways to ensure buy-in from senior leaders (CIPD, 2021). In doing so, it is clear how leadership is involved in LGBTQ+ networks developing organisations to support desired inclusive practices.

Furthermore, Leithwood et al. (2020) also reveal that more widely distributed school leadership has a greater influence on schools and students, and that teachers report being more committed to school leadership when leadership responsibilities are in-line with expertise. LGBTQ+ educators, through heightened awareness and their own experiences, often hold expertise in relation to LGBTQ+ inclusion and diversity, equity and inclusion more broadly. Distributing the leadership of these areas to LGBTQ+ networks could help to have a greater influence on the school and students, result in more commitment from the teachers themselves and help to develop members as leaders. However, some LGBTQ+ teachers discuss the challenge of being expected by senior leadership to speak on behalf of their entire community, or to lead on inclusion work internally without support or remuneration (Brett & Brassington, 2023). Senior leaders must be committed to supporting these networks, and if they are considering them as opportunities for leadership development, they must also consider what support and remuneration is available. This need not be solely financial – it could be protected time, training and professional development opportunities, or career progression. As research into distributed leadership suggests, 'new roles and responsibilities will inevitably emerge from an authentic distributed leadership model' (Leithwood et al., 2020, p. 14).

I started this chapter by telling you how I accidentally, through a desire for community, found myself co-leading an LGBTQ+ network. This work, although not a traditional leadership position, presented me with opportunities to develop confidence and competence in a variety of key leadership practices. Furthermore, it caused me to reimagine my understanding of what leadership can be. The more I explore this topic in my PhD research, I find myself wondering how powerful this could have been if I had entered with intention. If I had chosen to engage with LGBTQ+ networks not only for their social support or wider inclusion potential but also as a valuable opportunity for professional and leadership development. It is likely, based on the fact you are reading this book, that you yourself are interested in developing yourself as an LGBTQ+ leader. Or perhaps you are an ally considering ways to empower and support LGBTQ+ leadership in your setting. Either way, the chapters in this book will be full of inspiring ideas for you. It is my hope that this chapter has contributed to the ideas of this book by encouraging you to consider opportunities for developing leadership outside of the typical middle to senior leadership trajectory and to see involvement in LGBTQ+ networks as a valuable opportunity for developing leadership.

REFERENCES

Baker, P. (2022). *Outrageous: The story of Section 28 and Britain's battle for LGBT education* (1st ed.). Reaktion Books Ltd.

Beaver, G. R. (2023). Individual outcomes of employee resource group membership. *Personnel Review*, *52*(5), 1420–1436. https://doi.org/10.1108/PR-03-2021-0163

Brett, A. (2025). Space, surveillance, and stress: A lefebvrian analysis of heteronormative spatial production in schools, using a photo elicitation method with LGBT plus teachers. *Sex Education: Sexuality, Society and Learning*, *25*(2), 184–200. https://doi.org/10.1080/14681811.2023.2296473

Brett, A., & Brassington, J. (2023). *Pride & Progress: Making schools LGBT+ inclusive spaces*. Crowin.

CIPD. (2021). *A guide to establishing staff networks*. https://www.cipd.co.uk/Images/guide-to-establishing-staff-networks_tcm18-91862.pdf. (Einarsdóttir)

Colgan, F., Brook, P., Colgan, F., & McKearney, A. (2012). Visibility and voice in organisations. *Equality, Diversity and Inclusion: An International Journal*, *31*(4), 359–378. https://doi.org/10.1108/02610151211223049

Colgan, F., Creegan, C., McKearney, A., & Wright, T. (2006). *Lesbian, gay and bisexual workers: Equality, diversity and inclusion in the workplace?* Comparative Organisation and Equality Research Centre, London Metropolitan University. Available at: www.workinglives.org/londonmet/library/c85513_3.pdf

Colgan, F., & McKearney, A. (2012). Visibility and voice in organisations: Lesbian, gay, bisexual and transgendered employee networks. *Equality, Diversity and Inclusion: An International Journal, 31,* 359–378.

Dennissen, M., Benschop, Y., & den Brink, M. (2019). Diversity networks: Networking for equality? *British Journal of Management, 30*(4), 966–980. https://doi.org/10.1111/1467-8551.12321

Douglas, P. H. (2008). Affinity groups: Catalyst for inclusive organizations. *Employment Relations Today, 34*(4), 11–18. https://doi.org/10.1002/ert.20171

Githens, R. P., & Aragon, S. R. (2009). LGBT employee groups: Goals and organizational structures. *Advances in Developing Human Resources, 11,* 121–135.

Lee, C. (2020). Why LGBT teachers may make exceptional school leaders. *Frontiers in Sociology, 5,* 50. https://doi.org/10.3389/fsoc.2020.00050

Lee, C. (2023). *Pretended: Schools and section 28.* John Catt.

Leithwood, K., & Azah, V. (2016). Characteristics of effective leadership networks. *Journal of Educational Administration, 54*(4), 409–433.

Leithwood, K., Harris, A., & Hopkins, D. (2008). Seven strong claims about successful school leadership. *School Leadership & Management, 28*(1), 27–42. https://doi.org/10.1080/13632430701800060

Leithwood, K., Harris, A., & Hopkins, D. (2020). Seven strong claims about successful school leadership revisited. *School Leadership & Management*, *40*(1), 5–22. https://doi.org/10.1080/13632434.2019.1596077

LGBT Foundation. (2023). *Hidden Figures: The impact of the Covid-19 pandemic on LGBT communities in the UK.* https://lgbt.foundation/wp-content/uploads/2023/12/Hidden20Figures-20The20Impact20of20the20Covid-19 20Pandemic20on20on20LGBT20Communities.pdf

McFadden, C., & Crowley-Henry, M. (2018). 'My People': The potential of LGBT employee networks in reducing stigmatization and providing voice. *International Journal of Human Resource Management*, *29*(5), 1056–1081. https://doi.org/10.1080/09585192.2017.1335339

McFadden, C., Gedro, J. A., & Rocco, T. S. (2024). Breaking the mold or making the mold? LGBTQ employee networks and the managerialist agenda. In *The Routledge handbook of LGBTQ identity in organizations and society* (1. udg., s. 491–499). Routledge. https://doi.org/10.4324/9781003128151-39

Meyer, I. H. (2003). Prejudice, social stress, and mental health in lesbian, gay, and bisexual populations: Conceptual issues and research evidence. *Psychological Bulletin*, *129*(5), 674.

Perales, F. (2022). Improving the wellbeing of LGBTQ+ employees: Do workplace diversity training and ally networks make a difference? *Preventive Medicine*, *161*, 107113. https://doi.org/10.1016/j.ypmed.2022.107113

Raeburn, N. C. (2004). *Changing corporate America from inside out: Lesbian and gay work-place rights.* University of Minnesota Press.

3

NAVIGATING LEADERSHIP WITHOUT A MAP: A TRANS EDUCATOR'S JOURNEY IN EARLY YEARS

KELSEY-ANN CALDOW

LEAP Sports Scotland, UK

Keywords: Trans and non-binary identities; early years education; early years leadership; LGBTIQ+ inclusion; authentic leadership; inclusion

LEADERSHIP IN THE EARLY YEARS

At the time of writing, I am coming up on 10 years since I started working in Early Years. I began as an apprentice working with children aged six weeks to five years. Upon qualifying as an Early Years Practitioner, I continued working while studying towards a BA (Hons) in Childhood and Youth Studies. I then completed a Postgraduate degree in Primary Teaching and, after my probation year, returned to Early Years as a Nursery Teacher.

Being a Nursery Teacher differs significantly from the role of a Class Teacher. While you are there to support the learning, teaching and assessment of the learners, you also support Early Years Practitioners in the setting, often becoming an unrecognised middle leader in the process.

Within the context of a Nursery Teacher, leadership works best through a holistic approach. Leadership is not just about managing practitioners or overseeing a curriculum but it is about creating a nurturing, inclusive and supportive environment, and overall ethos where all learners, families and staff members can thrive. This is an effective approach as being my authentic self in the workplace sets a tone of safety and inclusion for all, encouraging others to do the same.

For me, queer and authentic leadership theory work harmoniously together, as just being your authentic self can challenge heteronormative assumptions. LaRocco and Bruns (2013) outlined four key themes of authentic leadership as one who can utilise their experiences for a shared purpose; participates in continuous learning; develops positive relationships; and models good practice. For me, this aligned with my own leadership style, to lead with empathy and openness to get to know others lived experiences, and work to develop and utilise the skillset within a team.

AUTHENTICITY IN LEADERSHIP

I have had mixed reactions to my being openly queer, particularly as a teacher. I was once told, 'Watch how you dress, you look like a lesbian' – they clearly didn't know me very well! This was several years ago and I can reflect and laugh at the ridiculousness of it now, because what does a lesbian even look like? But at the time, I was made to feel shame for expressing myself, so would wear make-up every day, opting for more feminine clothes. I went for interviews in this disguise and was unsuccessful. The first time I was successful in an interview, I wore my 'lesbian-look'. By being my authentic self, I was able to relax and be myself, and that interview brought me back into Early Years.

Recognising that authenticity was, in part, a key to my success. I made the decision to be myself at work. I laced up my brogues, buttoned up my shirt and started my job as a Nursery Teacher. Within a year, I came out to my nursery team as trans non-binary and was open to their questions, which were respectful and came from a place of wanting to understand my experience. My line manager supported my transition and helped me come out to my colleagues within the school and cluster. My experience of coming out and changing my pronouns to they/them was mostly positive, and I was given the opportunity to come out at my own pace and comfort level.

However, complications arose when I began using the gender-neutral title Mx. Within the school system, Mx was not an option, so the school admin enquired about this and was told to put my title as unknown. However, this meant the weekly register was headed with 'Unknown Caldow', so the title was changed back and tipex-ed over each week. After several emails from admin, the system was updated to have Mx as a recognised title. The nursery also updated their welcome board to now feature the pronouns of staff who wished to share their pronouns. This act of narrative leadership, though it seemed small, has allowed families to share their experiences with the setting, being open about identities and sharing that it made them feel more welcome. Furthermore, it demonstrates allyship within the team, an aspect of activism and advocacy that is all the more crucial within the current climate.

Since becoming Mx Caldow, the children have accepted this and for those who were curious, I tell them that I'm not really a man or a woman, just somewhere in-between so that's why I use Mx and they/them pronouns. While this is a grossly oversimplified definition of non-binary, my learners have understood it and are advocators on my behalf, correcting others when misgendering me. In a similar way that Butler (1990) refers to gender and identity as performative, leadership could also be viewed as a performance, led by the context we work within. As LGBTIQ+ leaders, we can make conscious decisions to shape the environment and model inclusive practice, demonstrating the potential a setting has for inclusion of marginalised or underrepresented identities.

CREATING MIRRORS AND WINDOWS

As educators, I feel it is our duty to create windows and mirrors in education (Style, 1988). To develop an inclusive curriculum, educators create mirrors where learners see themselves reflected in their education, relating to their identity, family and background. This then creates windows for learners to look outwards and see the diversity within their community, and wider society. I believe that by having opportunities to do so in Early Years, we can act as an early intervention to help prevent discrimination as they grow.

When I started, our Improvement Plan focused on Diversity and Inclusion. This was perfect, as the team had already recognised a lack of diversity in resources and were keen to make the change. As a new leader, getting to know the staff and understand their knowledge of diversity and inclusion was the first step in this journey, with practitioners having varied understanding of diversity, and how that would look in an Early Years setting. With this knowledge, through distributive leadership I was then able to utilise the skills we already had within the setting to allow for opportunities to lead from within the team.

This created a shared understanding of the importance of diversity and inclusion, linking to the UNCRC Rights of the Child, as well as the protected characteristics from the Equality Act (2010). This helped develop a wider picture of inclusion to then be able to consider what windows we had to advance for our learners to see themselves. We also carried out a book audit and realised that despite having a diverse demographic of families in the setting, the books we had available did not reflect that.

So, we changed our books, consulted with families and asked them to share their experiences and backgrounds, and we found that learners became more engaged and confident to share from their home lives and experiences. This did not happen overnight; it was a long process and one we are still changing and developing as the demographic and needs within our setting continues to evolve.

Furthermore, I feel my presence as an LGBTIQ+ educator has led to a cultural shift within the nursery and the wider school setting which we are a part of. Staff have shared how they are more aware of the language they use, not just in my presence but with learners, working towards using more gender-neutral language. As I have always been quite open about my identity, my colleagues know they are free to ask questions about my experiences, I feel my openness and authenticity about my identity has empowered my colleagues to ask questions about my LGBTIQ+ experiences. I have also had the opportunity to support teachers within the school to deliver lessons with LGBTIQ+ themes embedded, and signposting to available resources. This was carried out with support from my senior leadership team as part of a transformative leadership approach, underpinned by Fullan's (2007) approach to create a culture of change. This approach also ensures consistency within learning, where their understanding develops along a strand from nursery to the end of primary, with all practitioners working towards the same approach and outcomes, at appropriate levels for the learners.

EARLY INTERVENTIONS: DRAWING NEW ROUTES FROM THE TRADITIONAL NARRATIVES

The beauty of working in the Early Years is that we, as practitioners, have the opportunity to act as an early intervention for thinking within the traditional, binary narratives. I am a true believer in early intervention. I feel that if we begin to challenge learners thinking within the Early Years and offer them a broader understanding of the world around them, they can start to think critically about ideas that have been given to them and consider alternatives. What this looks like in practice is open, nurturing spaces where learners have the chance to explore and be curious, and our role as leaders and practitioners is to support learners to do so.

This quote by Sarah Keyworth (11 November 2020) eloquently sums up what we are trying to achieve in Early Years through early intervention.

> *There's this sort of irrational fear that the removal of gender stereotyping is the removal of fun, and the desire to limit what children are allowed to experience, when in fact it is the complete opposite. Making things gender neutral is simply making every item of clothing, every toy, every colour, an option for every child.*

And with current discourses in the media, that fear is very real and there are concerns that children are exposed to topics that remove their sense of childhood innocence. Of course, this is not the case, and what early intervention achieves is more opportunities for children to engage in childhood, a childhood without fear or judgement and a childhood where they can explore and be curious in a safe, nurturing environment.

THE IMPACT OF LEADERSHIP

From my work focusing on inclusion in the Early Years, I was selected as a Pedagogy Pioneer to deliver a webinar entitled 'Developing LGBTIQ+ Inclusion in the Early Years', delivered online to fellow Early Years Practitioners across Scotland, as well as a recording created to share with those unable to attend. Creating and delivering this webinar allowed me the opportunity to reflect on what LGBTIQ+ inclusion means within an Early Years context. I consulted with my deputy head to ensure the content was appropriate and informative, and his feedback was very positive and supportive. For him, this approach was about Family Inclusion, to show learners all the ways people can be a family, and that it is about the love that makes a family, not the genders. In my experience, collaborating with allies and with the LGBTIQ+ community can be beneficial to explore areas that may require further explanation or some adaptation. Making use of allyship in leadership is a key component and links back to authentic leadership (LaRocco & Bruns, 2013).

Within Early Years, even as young as three years old, I have seen boys shy away from dressing-up clothes, particularly if they are pink, but when a male member of staff engages in dress-up that would be considered traditionally feminine, those same boys will join in and engage with their role play, because they can see that barrier being brought down. When I deliver training in Early Years on LGBTIQ+ inclusion the focus is often on challenging gender stereotypes as this then takes away an assumption of the roles 'men' and 'women' play in society, allowing children to realise that they can be whoever they want to be, an important message for them to hear.

For me delivering as a Pedagogy Pioneer, I received feedback which gave me confidence and recognition that I was a leader and able to make change. Our Quality Improvement Officer for Early Years had watched the training and thanked me for delivering the training and referred to it as 'powerful' and noted that he had added his pronouns to his email signature, to show support and understanding of inclusive language and diverse gender identities. While this may seem like a small gesture, this was impactful to me as a trans person, and it gave me further insight to what leadership can look like in many forms.

I don't think I ever truly saw myself as a leader until I became a Nursery Teacher, as I had always thought of leadership through a structure of hierarchy, and leaders sat at the top, where I was not. I have since learnt that everyone has the potential to be a leader, our staff, our learners and our families. For me, a good leader sees the potential and skills in those around them, and homes in on and develops this to infuse these skills into the setting for the benefit of all. It's about knowing when to speak, when to listen and empower distributive leadership opportunities for both colleagues and learners.

SELF-CARE IN LEADERSHIP

Being a visibly queer, trans educator and leader in Early Years education requires a unique blend of resilience, authenticity and emotional labour. The work involves not only educating young children but also challenging societal norms, advocating for inclusive practices and often navigating complex and sometimes difficult conversations around identity and gender. As such, self-care is essential for maintaining both personal well-being and professional effectiveness. It is easy to become so immersed in activism and the daily demands of the role, that you can forget to care for your own needs. However, taking time to recharge is a necessity.

This was an important lesson I had to learn for myself. Alongside my role as a Nursery Teacher, I am an activist and youth worker within the LGBTIQ+ community, and the lines between professional and personal often blend together. However, I have come to realise setting clear boundaries between work and personal time is essential for wellbeing. While I take a lot of pleasure and empowerment from my activism work and being surrounded by the LGBTIQ+ community, I also have had to ensure there's space for relaxation, creative pursuits and simply being away from the responsibilities of teaching. It's also important to have access to affirming mental health support, in order to process the emotional weight of both personal and professional challenges in a safe, non-judgemental space.

As a queer educator, self-care for me also involves connecting with other LGBTIQ+ educators for mutual support and solidarity, knowing that I am not alone in navigating the complexities of my identity in the workplace. Accessing networks of teachers who are LGBTIQ+, or allies has had a significant impact on my own wellbeing, as I have never worked in a school with another openly LGBTIQ+ person.

Engaging with other LGBTIQ+, particularly trans and non-binary educators, helped to remove a sense of isolation; that I was not the only one.

For me, the importance of self-care is not just about maintaining personal well-being – it is also about sustaining the energy I need to continue the important work of activism and advocacy, both within and outside the Early Years setting. Being a queer leader in education often means acting as a representative and a visible source of support for both children and colleagues. By allowing myself time to recharge, I can return to work with renewed passion and clarity, ready to confront the challenges of both systemic and personal barriers while staying committed to the ongoing fight for visibility, inclusion and equity. Ultimately, self-care enables us, as queer and trans educators, to lead from a place of strength, balance and resilience, ensuring we can continue the important work both in the setting and as activists outside of it.

STAYING AUTHENTIC IN LEADERSHIP

In my leadership journey, I realised that the most important part of being a leader is authenticity. Being able to be open and honest about my experiences, not just as a queer person but also as an educator, I feel has made me a better leader and all round educator. I reflect on roles where I had not brought my whole self, and these are the jobs that I mull over and think about what I would have done differently.

Being an educator is as much a part of my identity as being LGBTIQ+, and I cannot be one without being the other, as well as all the other aspects of my identity that come together to make me, me. I would like to finish my chapter with a message I received from a parent not long after I came out as trans non-binary within my Early Years setting.

'My child and I have been talking a lot about gender and gender-neutral titles/identification, because you are Mx. Now some of her stuffies are they/them not he or she. Thought you might like to know. She is so interested in it and how to address people correctly and kindly'.

As a leader, that is the message that I always want to share, that regardless of identity, my learners will always treat people correctly and kindly. I think this shows the impact which LGBTIQ+ leadership has and emphasises the need to be open and authentic within your role. For me leadership is about stepping up and stepping out, and bringing your colleagues, learners and families along with you. It's about modelling inclusive practice and spotlighting these moments and also recognising where improvements are required. It's about being open to new learning, being able to listen and collaborate, and in the end, ensure the best outcomes for our learners.

REFERENCES

Butler, J. (1990). Gender trouble, feminist theory, and psychoanalytic discourse. In L. Nicholson (Ed.), *Feminism/postmodernism*. Routledge.

Fullan, M. (2007). *Leading in a culture of change*. John Wiley & Sons.

Keyworth, S. (2020) *Are you a boy or a girl? Season 1, Episode 1*, BBC Radio 4, 2020, November 11.

LaRocco, D. J., & Bruns, D. A. (2013). It's not the "What," it's the "How" four key behaviors for authentic leadership in early intervention. *Young Exceptional Children*, *16*(2), 33–44.

Style, E. (1988). *Curriculum as window and mirror*. Listening for All Voices. Available at: https://nationalseedproject.org/Key-SEED-Texts/curriculum-as-window-and-mirror

4

NAVIGATING LEADERSHIP AND LGBTQ+ VISIBILITY IN PRIMARY EDUCATION: REFLECTIONS ON SECTION 28, ADVOCACY AND INCLUSIVE PRACTICES

HOLLY COULL

Rise Multi-Academy Trust, UK

Keywords: LGBTQ+ leadership; primary education; Section 28 legacy; authentic leadership; inclusive school culture; minority stress in education

In this chapter, I reflect on my experiences as a queer leader in primary education, shaped by the legacy of Section 28—legislation that for years silenced LGBTQ+ visibility in schools. Although fully repealed in 2003, it contributed to the fears and complexities I encountered throughout my career, navigating my identity within a professional context. I explore how invisibility, fear and societal attitudes have shaped both my identity and my leadership, and how understanding this context has allowed me to advocate for greater inclusivity and representation.

DISCOVERING SECTION 28

Throughout my entire life, education has been at the core of my experiences—as a student from primary school to university, then as a primary school teacher, a headteacher and now as a teaching and learning lead. Yet, it was only a few years ago that I first encountered Section 28. At the time, I was a headteacher and engaged to be married when I listened to the podcast, 'Out with Suzi Ruffell', where she discussed legislation that had shaped her schooling. As she reflected on its impact, I realised that my own educational journey had been similarly affected. How had I never learnt about this? How could such a significant aspect of my schooling have remained hidden throughout my entire education? Determined to understand more, I learnt that Section 28 was in effect in England from 1988 to 2003. Having started school in 1989 and completed my secondary education in 2002, this legislation had been in place for my entire school life. It had prevented local authorities from 'promoting homosexuality' but it was not clear exactly what this meant for schools. If you were a gay teacher, would that mean you could lose your job? If a child came to you for support about being queer, could you help them? This created uncertainty in schools, leaving teachers unsure about what they were permitted to discuss, both within the curriculum and when sharing aspects of their personal lives with colleagues. Due to Section 28, there was no representation of LGBTQ+ individuals in my education; the only references to LGBTQ+ identities were whispered speculations about who might be a lesbian. These were never positive discussions; they were whispered secrets. Section 28 might have been lifted in 2003 but nearly 20 years on it was still having an impact on me.

This revelation was pivotal in helping me understand the feelings I had harboured regarding my identity as a queer individual and as a queer school leader. I was uncertain what shocked me more—the existence of Section 28 itself or the fact that I had remained unaware of it for so long. This realisation helped me to understand that navigating my queerness as a headteacher had added complexity to an already demanding role. I constantly questioned whether, and how, I could be my true self whilst navigating my new role as headteacher. Suzi Ruffell (2024) quoted Marian Wright Edelman on her podcast by saying 'You can't be what you can't see'. It would take another year before I encountered a school leader who helped me understand how my queerness could support my leadership style.

EARLY LEADERSHIP

When I started my role as headteacher, I hadn't been confidently queer in my personal life for long. However, I was now engaged to be married, which meant I wanted to talk about my soon-to-be wife all the time! That created even more of a struggle when I spoke to parents and children. The people I worked with knew I was queer, but the wider school community didn't. Working in a Church of England school added another layer of anxiety for me. Would parents question my ability to lead because of my identity? Fortunately, my CEO, fellow headteachers and the Director of Education, who was openly gay, did not share this concern. For the first time, I witnessed a gay leader in education navigating their professional life while being fully themselves. However, I still lacked a roadmap for how to integrate my professional and personal identities. A conversation with the Director of Education helped me understand that, in some schools, his sexuality was known, while in others, it was not—a personal decision based on context. I recognised that I, too, had agency over how I discussed my identity in different environments. I knew I thrived when I could be my authentic self, a concept central to George's (2003) assertion that authentic leadership is grounded in self-awareness and remaining true to one's values and identity. Yet, I also understood that there was no universal approach.

Policy Development

One aspect of my new role I found challenging was the development of policies and this was especially true for the Relationships and Sex Education policy. I frequently sought reassurance from colleagues because I feared that my queer identity would lead others to assume I was imposing an agenda, even though I was still keeping this part of me a secret. After many conversations with supportive colleagues, they helped me remember that the policy was statutory, and I wasn't doing anything different from anyone else in the Trust. This meant I could be more confident to introduce books that included LGBTQ+ characters or tell related stories in collective worship. Consequently, I finally felt confident enough to lead a collective worship session on Pride Month. To my relief, it was received without controversy. I felt proud knowing that students in my school were learning about Pride Month—something that had been entirely absent from my own education. Consequently, we expanded our library to include books featuring LGBTQ+ characters, taking steps towards representation and inclusivity. When I heard children talk about books with two dads or read a book about going to Pride, it always made me smile. I wondered how different my life would have been if I had read books like this growing up. Working in primary schools, I used to worry that if I told children I was queer or used a topic around pride, I would be the first person to talk about such topics. I know that every child will learn about age-appropriate LGBTQ+ topics from the age of four, and if they haven't yet, then I am allowed to teach them what pride is or what I mean by queer without worrying about repercussions.

During Pride Month, I started to wear a pride pin badge, I knew that even if I was not fully open about my identity, the badge would signal my support for LGBTQ+ visibility. I recall a student noticing it and complimenting it. In that moment, I questioned whether I should explain its significance or disclose my identity I hadn't been in a position before that a pupil had asked about my sexuality, so I had not ever lied to them. However, I'd never chosen to disclose the information. Ultimately, at that time, I didn't think it was appropriate. I realised that my hesitation stemmed from the societal conflation of homosexuality with sex itself. This hesitation speaks to the problematic nature of LGBTQ+ teacher visibility, which can be a source of vulnerability within educational spaces. Yet, as Brett (2022) discusses, there are also benefits and opportunities that can arise from being an openly LGBTQ+ teacher, offering moments of solidarity and representation for students. All I might have said was, 'I have a girlfriend' or 'I'm queer'—statements entirely separate from discussions of sex. Although the student understood the meaning of the badge, I wondered if that would have been an opportunity to tell a student. What if telling them could have had a positive impact on their life? However, the fear of the repercussions meant I didn't.

Trust-wide Advocacy

After two years as a headteacher, I started a new role as a teaching and learning lead within the Trust and got married during the summer. Upon returning, I loved my new title—Mrs Coull—and loved each opportunity I got to share that I had a wife. This change felt easier to share which allowed me to express my identity with newfound confidence. In my new role, working across multiple schools, I often mentioned my wife to colleagues. I knew how happy and confident my wife made me, and because I saw people less frequently, I worried less about whether they had negative thoughts about my sexuality. I also hoped that by being confident in who I am, I could help others feel more comfortable with their own identity. The main difference was that I was no longer in charge of a specific school and therefore did not have direct interactions with parents or children. I no longer had casual conversations with families about the weekend, limiting opportunities to talk about my wife despite my increased confidence. When working with a group of students, a few months into my new role, one child asked if Mrs Coull meant that I was married. Yes, I said. To whom they asked. To my wife, I replied. This marked the first occasion I openly identified as queer to a student. After that, the child smiled and returned to their work, and there was no subsequent discussion. The years of anxiety surrounding my identity ending with simple acknowledgement, leading to a sense of relief as nothing negative transpired.

After stepping down from my role as headteacher, I recognised how my fear of how the parents at the school might react, had added a complexity to the already demanding role. During a lecture by Dr Adam Brett, I learned about the concept of 'minority stress' (Meyer, 2003) and the substantial mental burden it imposed on me. In the simplest of conversations with a parent, there was always a part of me that was thinking about my identity and the 'what ifs' of them finding out. I wanted to be open about my identity, but I wasn't.

Looking back, I regret not disclosing my queerness, as I wonder whether it could have supported a child or a parent navigating their own identity.

Pride at Rise

As my confidence grew, I became more vocal about my identity and how we could learn from experiences like mine. As I began discussing potential changes, I started attending the Diversity, Equality and Inclusion (DEI) meetings we were undertaking as a Trust. It was an eye-opening experience. In our first session, we discussed which of the nine protected characteristics we'd feel comfortable sharing with a stranger. I shared how, when a stranger once told me that homosexuality was a sin, I didn't feel safe to respond. For some people at the table, it was a surprise to learn that there were people with such reactions to homosexuality, but it taught them that aspects of your life sometimes aren't freely shared. Talking with my group helped me realise the importance of educating people within my Trust to ensure all our schools were places where people felt they could be themselves and were safe to do so. In that session, we identified areas for improvement. I chose staff experiences, reinforced by earlier discussions. Realising I couldn't reach everyone across our 20 schools, I created a newsletter, 'Pride at Rise', for LGBT+ History Month, complete with a pride version of our logo. It was a small, meaningful start.

Once the newsletter was shared, I awaited the reactions. It included my story, the rationale behind my writing, and recommendations for LGBTQ+ books. Shortly after someone approached me to discuss the newsletter. All my previous thoughts led me to fear a negative response. However, I was met with gratitude. The individual expressed how transformative it would have been for them to have had teachers who openly discussed LGBTQ+ topics during their own schooling. It confirmed the importance of my newsletter as a vehicle for change. I recognised that change doesn't need to start with grand actions but can begin with small, impactful steps, like writing the 'Pride at Rise' newsletter. As Bass and Avolio (1994) highlight, effective leadership involves using one's influence to guide others towards meaningful change, often starting with modest initiatives that set the tone for larger movements.

Over the next term, we held our first in-person 'Pride at Rise' meeting, and the newsletters continued. I had conversations that likely wouldn't have happened without it. Growing more comfortable discussing my wife in the staffroom, I noticed ongoing anxiety about such discussions in classrooms. Some heterosexual colleagues, unaware of these complexities, didn't realise the challenges LGBTQ+ individuals face when sharing personal details. They were surprised that some LGBTQ+ individuals could speak confidently in the staffroom, but that confidence didn't carry over to the classroom. This may be due to feelings of shame, stemming from the lack of role models, derogatory comments about homosexuality or the silence that allows harmful assumptions to go unchallenged. When I was a headteacher, there were so many Monday mornings when families would talk to me about their weekend. There was often a moment I would need to pause and decide what I would say. If I was telling them what I'd done, I'd always stop short of telling them who I'd gone with. Looking back now, there were so many opportunities that I could have added into a conversation that I went with my girlfriend, but I didn't. Instead, I overanalysed every interaction, carefully considering what I could or should say and always deciding that I should not tell children of my queerness. As I explained to the people in the staffroom about Section 28, they started to realise why there can be a fear about sharing personal information with children. Staff began to understand why LGBTQ+ individuals tell different versions of their stories to different people, even within the same context. Staff recognised that a fear still existed among LGBTQ+ individuals that sharing personal information might be perceived as promoting their sexuality, despite it being decades since the legislation had ended.

Widening Impact and Embedding Change

Since launching the 'Pride at Rise' newsletter, I have joined the Trust's DEI working party for the Trust, where we are now positioned to enact meaningful change. My small step—sharing my newsletter—has evolved into a collective effort to influence policy and incorporate diverse perspectives across the Trust. Recently, I presented the DEI strategy at our leadership forum, ensuring that all school leaders within the trust were aware of our initiatives. I shared my story and the work we are doing, articulating my deep-seated passion for fostering change. One story I shared is the anxiety surrounding the equality questions in job applications. I remember the fear of having to disclose my sexuality if I sought a new position. Should I lie on an application? Years ago, very few people in my life knew I was queer, which meant lying on application form seemed possible. But what if I told the truth? Would that prevent me from securing a role, particularly in a Church of England school? I explained the fear about equality questions because many individuals have not faced such dilemmas and may not recognise the potential obstacles that others encounter. Reflecting on my former self, fearful of completing application forms, I now find myself in a position to effect change. My experiences inform my efforts to create a more inclusive environment, helping to ensure that others do not endure the same fears I once faced. As Lee (2020) highlights, having experienced exclusion and marginalisation, LGBTQ+ teachers often develop a heightened empathy and are highly sensitised to inclusive best practice, both within their classrooms and among their colleagues. In turn, the positive outcomes of these changes extend beyond the LGBTQ+ community, fostering a culture of inclusivity that benefits all.

The Lessons I Have Learnt

As a queer leader in education, I continue to navigate the shadows of Section 28 and the complexities of identity in professional spaces. I have learnt that visibility matters—you can't be what you can't see—and that the absence of role models can shape our sense of what is possible. The legacy of historical prejudice lingers long after laws are repealed, and it takes conscious, compassionate leadership to recognise and address those hidden echoes. I have discovered that leadership is a deeply personal, often courageous journey, where small acts, like a newsletter or a badge, can quietly spark cultural shifts. Courage does not always mean loud declarations; it sometimes lies in wise, context-sensitive decisions about when and how to be visible. I have seen the power of lived experience in driving organisational change, and how personal stories can inform inclusive leadership. My hope is that these lessons offer encouragement and guidance to others navigating their own journeys of identity, leadership and change.

REFERENCES

Bass, B. M., & Avolio, B. J. (1994). *Improving organizational effectiveness through transformational leadership.* Sage Publications.

Brett, A. (2022). *Under the spotlight: Exploring the challenges and opportunities of being a visible LGBT+ teacher.* Sex Education. https://doi.org/10.1080/14681811.2022.2143344

George, B. (2003). *Authentic leadership: Rediscovering the secrets to creating lasting value.* Jossey-Bass.

Lee, C. (2020). Why LGBT teachers may make exceptional school leaders. *Frontiers in Sociology, 5,* 50. https://doi.org/10.3389/fsoc.2020.00050

Meyer, I. H. (2003). Prejudice, social stress, and mental health in lesbian, gay, and bisexual populations: Conceptual issues and research evidence. *Psychological Bulletin, 129*(5), 674–697.

Ruffell, S. (2024). *Out with Suzi Ruffell' podcast.* Available at https://podcasts.apple.com/gb/podcast/out-with-suzi-ruffell/id1505466130

5

A QUIET ACTIVISM: HOW MY EXPERIENCE AS AN LGBT+ TEACHER AND LEADER SHAPES MY DRIVE FOR CHANGE IN SCHOOLS

GERLINDE ACHENBACH

GAEd, UK

Keywords: LGBT+ inclusion in primary schools; relationships and sex education; activism; Section 28; authenticity

CAN YOU TEACH ABOUT GAY PEOPLE?

"Can you teach about gay people to six and seven year olds?" asks a Year 2 primary teacher. As a consultant in LGBT+ Inclusion, working with schools, I'm often asked questions like this. I would love to say, that the guidance from leaders at both school and government levels is comprehensive enough for an answer to be found simply by turning to a particular page in a specific document. I would love the answer to be an easy 'yes'. Instead, the question hangs, like a piñata, ready to be batted this way and that, depending on to whom you're talking. It represents the uncertainty felt by many colleagues in school settings who are, quite simply, unsure exactly what can and can't be taught. In one way, the question is symptomatic of a society which feels increasingly hostile and intolerant to difference. In another, it is the historic legacy of Section 28 (1988–2003).

SECTION 28

I came out to myself as lesbian in my mid-twenties, knowing that I felt increasingly uncomfortable trying to be 'straight'. This was in 1988. That same year, I became a primary teacher and Section 28 came into law. During this period, the 'gay and lesbian' community (as it was known then) existed in a climate of hate and fearmongering around AIDS and paedophilia encouraged by homophobic press coverage (Strudwick, 2019). In schools we were fearful that simply being lesbian or gay could be seen as promoting homosexuality and lead to instant dismissal. Many focused on teaching well, maintaining an impeccable professional record, and hiding their personal lives from colleagues. Those of us who chose to pursue leadership positions did so knowing the risks of increased visibility. The threat of being 'outed' meant living in a state of constant vigilance, covering tracks and arranging heteronormative alibis with friends.

Within a few years I met my long-term partner. We taught in the same primary school. We couldn't be 'out' about our relationship and people suspected us from the start. Looking back, it's hard to know how much the suspicion was simply curiosity or blatant homophobia, fuelled by the media view that we were unnatural or perverted. As soon as we started to live together, my partner and I had to pretend that we weren't: we got an additional phone line installed at home so that we could give the school office two separate contact numbers; when driving home we were careful that we weren't being followed, as sometimes we were; when we went supermarket shopping, we took two individual trolleys so that we could legitimately separate should we be spotted by families or colleagues. It was a time of great joy and extreme vigilance.

As teachers, our professional behaviour had to be impeccable. We gave 100% of our energy to the school and were recognised as 'outstanding' in our respective roles. We would talk about needing to 'make sure we had enough in the bank' (enough respect, appreciation) in case of a huge abandonment if people 'found out'. Being found out meant facing public rejection, humiliation or the loss of our jobs.

Despite the difficulties, we decided that we wanted to have a family. Our reality was that we were closeted lesbians, working in a local authority school during Section 28. We were surrounded by children yet prohibited from having our own. Spurred on by the barriers we faced, we determined to claim our equal right to be parents, together. At the time, in London, the Pregnancy Advisory Service was supporting single women, including lesbians, with donor insemination. Sadly, we were not able to be recognised as a couple. We played the game, presenting as a 'single' woman with a very supportive, close friend.

Once our first child was on the way, my partner pre-empted anyone 'discovering' the news. As Headteacher, she quietly told the staff and governors at school. Fortunately, their response was largely positive and showed us that, yes, we had enough 'in the bank'. My experience wasn't so positive. Now in a new school, with new colleagues, I found myself isolated in a senior role and unsure about how open I could be. There were no signs that it was safe, no posters, messaging, policy statements or supportive leaders. I used the gender-neutral 'they' about my partner and did not return after maternity leave.

Our very different experiences characterise how schools operated at the time. It was almost impossible to be an 'out' lesbian or gay teacher unless you were already well known, liked and respected. Even then, the risk of being 'outed' by the wider community and finding yourself unemployed was significant, although it's worth noting that no teacher was ever prosecuted under Section 28. My partner took that risk at the time so that our child, our family, could exist equally and with pride. We were prepared to be role models for diversity and family difference in the schools in which we served and which our children subsequently attended. We didn't see ourselves as pioneers at the time but, looking back, I think we were. Was it an activism of sorts? I think so, a challenge to the law makers who dared to impose their prejudice and restrictions on people's lives and happiness.

AUTHENTICITY

The impact of Section 28 didn't just stop in 2003 when it was repealed. Lee (2023) describes how, since then, LGBT+ teachers have often chosen to keep their heads below the parapet. The introduction of the Equality Act in 2010 meant that schools were required—and, importantly, also had permission—to develop their inclusive approaches around the protected characteristics detailed in the Act, including sexual orientation and gender reassignment. Like many other LGBT+ teachers and school leaders, I was excited by the potential of this legislation but felt worried about the consequences of being 'exposed', post-Section 28.

The Equality Act empowered me to be authentically myself at work. It requires schools to support and protect LGBT+ pupils, staff and families. However, in my experience, schools and their communities are intransigent and slow to change, particularly where social 'norms' are concerned. Significantly, current data shows that, in contrast to other workplaces, schools are not deemed safe environments for LGBT+ members of staff to be authentically themselves. The charity organisation, Just Like Us, ran a survey in 2021 which found that only 37% of LGBT+ school staff believe a colleague would feel comfortable to come out in their workplace. This does not come as a surprise. Across my career, I have encountered many members of staff, including well-intentioned leaders, who find it hard to separate LGBT+ from sexual activity. As Lundin (2016, p. 69) describes, 'A heterosexual teacher can talk about a partner without being accounted for talking about sexuality, whereas the homo- or bisexual teacher is at risk of being understood as talking inappropriately about sexuality'.

TOO CONTROVERSIAL?

In turn, this has an impact on what is taught in schools. The Department for Education Relationships and Sex Education (RSE) and Health Education guidance tells primary schools they should, 'Ensure that the needs of all pupils are appropriately met, and that all pupils understand the importance of equality and respect' and 'Ensure that all of their (LGBT content teaching) is sensitive and age appropriate' (DfE, 2019, p. 15). This brings me back to the question posed by the Year 2 teacher at the start of this chapter. They ask where teaching about gay people fits into the Year 2 curriculum. In response, the Headteacher needs to consider the school's public sector equality duty to be inclusive of sexual orientation, as well as to consider age-appropriateness.

As a primary Head, I know that judging 'age appropriateness' can be one of the hardest things to do. Headteachers I work with tell me that, in such instances, the fear of angry parents queuing outside classroom doors can quickly reduce the positive image of a gay relationship to 'what happens in bed'. Making the judgement 'not age appropriate' can feel like the least controversial, and therefore easiest, decision. However, they tell me that they fight the impulse to do this and that they challenge it in others. They know that the Year 2 teacher does not need to talk about gay sex in order to teach children aged six and seven about the different kinds of relationships and families that exist in our world. They appreciate that the unhelpful trope linking LGBT+ to sex hinders understanding that being LGBT+ is about identity, culture and relationships.

As I have expanded my work into secondary education, I have seen how sexual orientation and gender reassignment continue to cause the greatest controversy in culture and curriculum review. However, pupil statistics from the Just Like Us (2021) survey tell us that almost half of LGBT+ pupils aged 11–18 say they don't feel safe at school and that one in five homophobic, biphobic and transphobic bullying incidents go unreported. These are worrying statistics. Schools choosing the least controversial routes and avoiding LGBT+ inclusion are not supporting LGBT+ pupils. However, those challenging the deemed 'controversy' and shaping it, distilling it into shared values, are making the biggest difference. Outcomes from the same survey are clear that, in schools where messaging about being LGBT+ is positive, the impact on the wellbeing of *all* pupils, not just LGBT+ pupils, is significant.

Culture shift is not a quick fix, nor is it solved by a series of bolt-ons. It is not about a tweak to policy wording or an annual pride assembly. Real culture change happens with a deep commitment, over time, to a programme of staff and governor training, an evaluation of systems, protocols and policies and a review of curriculum and classroom practice (Dellenty, 2019).

CHALLENGING THE SYSTEMS

Some describe a commitment to LGBT+ inclusion in schools as 'woke'. They say this with little direct experience of being LGBT+ in schools over the past four decades. Running a leadership and governor workshop on system review recently, I saw one of the governors roll their eyes when I introduced the concept of heteronormativity. I began, "Heteronormativity is the unspoken assumption that heterosexual relationships (that is, between a man and a woman) are 'normal' or 'expected' and other relationships are not." The governor shook their head and shifted in their seat while the other attendees looked down at their papers, embarrassed. I recall talking with my own governors in 2015 about carrying out an overhaul of school systems to ensure they were inclusive. Their response was nothing like this. There were no micro-aggressive eye rolls or pushback, just honest agreement that an inclusive system benefits everyone. If being 'woke' means being aware, let's all strive for wokeness.

My own experience of heteronormativity as a lesbian parent was to influence my first challenges as a new Headteacher. The heterosexual (and married) family has long been assumed in schools, with new applicants being asked for mother's and father's names, children being asked about their 'mum and dad', a tacit assumption that a single parent is straight. In fact, the heteronormative assumption is that all parents are straight and that all families fit the heterosexual mould. Heteronormativity and cisnormativity represent the accepted and unspoken norm, promoted through language, policy and practice (Brett & Brassington, 2023). Cisnormativity—the idea that identifying with the sex assigned to you at birth is assumed—is reinforced by gender defined pupil uniform and gendered staff dress codes. In my experience, such codes make little or no accommodation for gender diversity, trans identities or any autonomy in a school.

As a Head, I understood that no amount of system change—inclusive wording on application forms, a policy of inclusive uniform—would shift school culture on its own. I recognised that the *language* we use in schools on a day-to-day basis also has an influence on young people's identities, self-perception and ambition. We hear boys described as messy and noisy, girls as neat and quiet. In the playground, staff address girls as 'darling' and boys as 'mate'. We use heteronormative and binary phrases—'boys and girls', 'ladies and gentlemen'. In primary schools we see boys and girls separated by gender for all kinds of reasons and rarely because gender is the issue, for example, when we line children up or send them for a drink. Not only can this use of language and practice exclude trans, non-binary and gender diverse children and adults but it can serve to reaffirm gender inequalities between boys and girls. I encourage leaders to introduce a culture of 'think before you speak' in all interactions, asking staff at all levels to support each other in adopting neutral and inclusive words, phrases and practice.

Through culture change and by taking a strategic approach, we have the opportunity to challenge embedded assumptions and norms. As school leaders, our duty is to acknowledge the cultural shift needed in our individual organisations and begin to look at the inclusion of LGBT+ in the context of love, relationships, identity and family, indeed the very things that bind our communities together.

#BELONGING #REPRESENTATIONMATTERS

Twenty or so years on from being that young teacher working under Section 28, my experience helped set a bar for my own leadership. It kindled a determination to ensure that the schools I led were places where everyone could be themselves—every child, member of staff and member of the community. Values-led schools carry out a deep exploration of what matters to them, many citing 'belonging' as key. To belong is to feel acknowledged and accepted. It's the opposite of the experience I had in the early 1990s. Nowadays, if I see a representation of my own identity as a lesbian partner on, for example, a television advert, it matters to me: I see my authentic self in everyday life – shopping, attending a school concert. If an LGBT+ family sees themselves represented in a story that their child has brought home from school, on posters in their school's entrance hall or in the wording of a school prospectus, it matters to them. It matters for their child.

Schools have an even greater tool at their disposal to achieve this goal, the curriculum. Kara (2024, p. 1) describes it as 'the strongest, most powerful lever we have to construct a better sense of belonging for all'. For too long our curricula have represented the lives and views of 'great men' through history, invariably white and portrayed as undeniably heterosexual. Leaders in education have the power to create uniquely diverse curricula through a multitude of DEI lenses, ensuring that the voices and stories of the LGBT+ community are heard and 'usualised'.[1]

FOR THOSE COMING AFTER...

The phrase, 'You can't be what you can't see' is widely attributed to US civil rights and children's rights activist, Marian Wright Edelman. As a call for representation and role models, it works for all marginalised communities. When I consider the absence of LGBT+ representation and role modelling for young people during Section 28, I reflect upon how much we have moved on. The values-led school communities with which I work are a microcosm of the inclusive work being done by educators across the United Kingdom and beyond. However, there is no room for complacency. In this decade, the trans community is subject to similar hatred and vitriol experienced by lesbian and gay people in the 1980s and 1990s. In schools, we have a duty to consider the whole child, the whole person. By keeping their needs and best interests at heart we can play our part in weathering this storm, ensuring that our trans young people *can* be what they see, that our trans colleagues have a community and that all can belong.

Not long ago, I was invited to speak at the annual graduation ceremony for the Chartered College of Teaching. As a recently conferred 'Fellow', I wanted to convey my pride for the contribution I have been able to make to the profession. In preparation, I revisited those years under the shadow of Section 28, recalling the high professional standards to which

---

1 A term first used in 2007 by Professor Sue Sanders, founder of Schools OUT and LGBT + History Month.

I have always worked. I remembered being acutely aware, at that time, that others holding these same standards could, at any point, judge my personal life as reprehensible.

This experience affected my ability to be authentically myself until I was well into my career as a Headteacher and since then I have sought to destigmatise and de-marginalise the LGBT+ community in the schools in which I have worked. I want more for the LGBT+ teachers and leaders who come after me. I hope, through my work, to make a tangible difference to their experience and enable them to bring their whole selves to their profession with pride.

REFERENCES

Brett, A., & Brassington, J. (2023). *Pride & Progress: Making schools LGBT+ inclusive spaces*. Corwin.

Dellenty, S. (2019). *Celebrating difference, a whole school approach to LGBT+ inclusion*. Bloomsbury.

Department for Education. (2019). *Relationships education, relationships and sex education (RSE) and health education: Statutory guidance for governing bodies, proprieters, head teachers, principals, senior leadership teams, teachers*. Available at: http://assets.publishing.service.gov.uk/government/uploads/system/uploads/attachment_data/file/1090195/Relationships_Education_RSE_and_Health_Education.pdf

Just Like Us. (2021). Growing up LGBT+: The impact of school, home and coronavirus on LGBT+ young people. Available at: https://www.justlikeus.org/wp-content/uploads/2021/11/Just-Like-Us-2021-report-Growing-Up-LGBT.pdf

Kara, B. (2024). *The diverse curriculum*. Sage.

Lee, C. (2023). *Pretended: Schools and Section 28: Historical, cultural and personal perspectives*. John Catt.

Lundin, M. (2016). Homo- and bisexual teachers' ways of relating to the heteronorm. *International Journal of Educational Research*, *75*(75), 67–75. https://doi.org/10.1016/j.ijer.2015.11.005

Strudwick, P. (2019). *This man spent 25 years fighting newspapers over their anti-gay reporting and finally won*. BuzzFeed.News. https://www.buzzfeed.com/patrickstrudwick/this-man-spent-25-years-fighting-newspapers-over-their

Section 2

NAVIGATING LGBTQ+ LEADERSHIP: GOVERNANCE, SECONDARY AND FURTHER EDUCATION

6

REFLECTIONS AS A GAY LEADER IN UK SECONDARY SCHOOLS

RICHARD MCDONALD

The Education Alliance, UK

Keywords: LGBT+ leadership; LGBT+ leadership in secondary education; authenticity in leadership; professional identity; allyship; LGBT+ role models

OVERLAPPING IDENTITIES

In their book, Brett and Brassington (2023) discuss the nature of LGBT+ teachers' identities through the lens of Goffman's dramaturgy (Goffman, 1959), whereby we perform different roles based on the social contexts we find ourselves in. They explain that the relationships between personal and professional identities can be explored by considering the ways in which our teacher identity, colleague identity and personal identity overlap and differ. As a leader, I feel that a fourth element—leader identity – is introduced, as this role introduces a new identity that impacts the performance of a professional identity and how this might vary depending on any given situation (see Fig. 6.1).

LEADERSHIP OUTSIDE EDUCATION

Between my undergraduate degree and teaching, I spent a few years in the world of retail management. Working in retail alongside my degree, I had a gay manager who was proud to be gay, juxtaposing the shame that I—like many—felt after growing up in the 1990s.

It is no wonder, then, that as a manager myself, I felt secure in being openly gay at work. My personal and

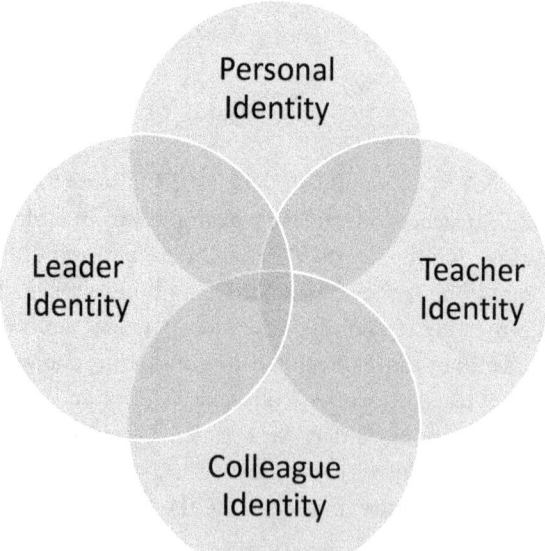

Fig. 6.1. Personal and Professional Identities. *Source:* **Adapted from Brett and Brassington (2023).**

colleague identities overlapped significantly. Due to this, the performance of my professional identity felt much less artificial as it incorporated so much of my authentic self.

BECOMING A TEACHER

The return to university (for a PGCE, Postgraduate Certificate in Education) and the less formal relationships with my fellow trainees meant that at university I felt able to be as authentic as I had been in retail. However, in my placement schools, I felt a need to hide being gay, a feeling shared by other LGBT+ teachers (Clarke, 1996; Endo et al., 2010; Khayatt & Iskander, 2019; Lee, 2019a; Litton, 2001; Weems, 1999). At the time, I was unaware of Section 28 of the Local Government Act, 1988 – much less the subtlety of its repeal (Lee, 2019b) – but I could clearly remember my own school experience.

At my secondary school, there were teachers who were known to be lesbian or gay, though it was implicit that it was not something to discuss publicly. I always had a sense that being gay or lesbian was something to be ashamed of. Given that Section 28 was in place until I was in sixth form, it is no surprise that cis-heteronormativity was reinforced by the curriculum and Personal, Social, Health and Economic Education (PSHE) in particular.

Likewise, as a trainee, I inferred that being gay was not something I should talk about or display in school. Though this was never explicitly stated through my training provider or staff in my placement schools, the regular reference to Part 2 of the Teachers' Standards (Department for Education, 2011), focusing on 'Professional Conduct', made me feel that my professional identity needed to be kept distant from my identity as a gay man. As a result, I felt that I could not truly be myself in school. This raises the question of what additional support LGBT+ trainees might need in navigating the relationship between their professional and personal identities, including advice on what being an out LGBT+ teacher could look like.

NEWLY QUALIFIED

As a newly qualified teacher (NQT), I worked alongside two lesbian women who showed me that my personal identity did not have to be at odds with who I would be at work. As with the participants in Brett et al.'s research (2024), this small network enabled me to feel a sense of solidarity and helped me feel more secure in the intersection of my own professional and personal identities. Whether they realised it or not, these role models gave me confidence in the ability to be myself in the classroom.

The approach I took at this stage very much aligned with Fenwick and Sanders' (2011) concept of *usualising*; I never made the deliberate decision to 'come out' to students but would mention my partner in passing (in the same way that I had seen heterosexual colleagues mention their families). One specific example I remember involved discussing the concept of marriage with a Year 9 class. When asked if I had a wife, I explained that I had a male partner, leading to a brief discussion of the recent law allowing same-sex marriage in England and Wales. Feeling comfortable to do this enabled me to find a stronger sense of authenticity. Butler's (1990) concept of performativity explores how gender and sexual orientation are something that we 'perform' through our actions and behaviours. In this sense, I was able to develop a performed identity at work that enabled a greater overlap between my teacher identity and personal identity, meaning that the role of teacher felt more authentically part of me as a person.

USUALISING AS A LEADER

I got my first leadership role in the same school that I had been in as an NQT. Consequently, I had a network of colleagues who I enjoyed working with alongside strong relationships with students. Across this time, I had no real desire to lead a Pride Group or have input on LGBT+ events (such as LGBT+ History Month or Pride Month). Professionally, my interests lay more in developing pedagogy and the English curriculum. Khayatt (1997) discusses this potential conflict between the teacher and personal identities, exploring the risk that all content taught by a teacher is then filtered through the lens of their LGBT+ identity. Likewise, despite being authentic by not hiding my sexuality from anyone at work, I still felt that being 'professional' meant not making my sexuality the main focus of any discussions with students, especially in the English classroom.

When I moved to a new school as a Director of English, I moved away from those colleagues who had helped me develop a professional identity that was authentically me. However, the confidence I had built in this meant that I felt able to continue using that professional identity in my new school (with both students and staff), despite not working with those colleagues. On reflection, I feel that the foundation of strong teacher and colleague identities at my previous school gave me the confidence in navigating this new role and integrating it into my professional identity overall. This is a sentiment reflected in Llewellyn and Reynolds (2021), where the positive reactions participants received when initially coming out enabled them to feel more at ease with being out later in their career.

However, despite feeling less of a focus on LGBT+ inclusion at this school, I still felt strongly that I wanted my presence as a gay teacher and leader to be usualising the presence of a gay person working in a school. In retrospect, I am unsure whether this approach was too subtle. Fletcher (2022) argues that LGBT+ teacher role models enable LGBT+ students to feel a sense of belonging and support, but was me being present enough to ensure this?

FINDING MY PLACE

The launch of the *Pride & Progress* podcast in 2021 (Brassington & Brett, 2021) marked a transformative moment for me. Listening to the diverse voices of LGBT+ educators helped me situate my own reality within the broader context of LGBT+ experience. Discussing the podcast with colleagues also became a catalyst for acts of allyship—most notably from the headteacher at that time, who was also my line manager. He moved beyond surface-level endorsement, actively exploring LGBT+ issues in whole-staff spaces, which signalled a commitment to inclusion that was both visible and meaningful. Research suggests that such intentional gestures of allyship, particularly when initiated by leadership, are more powerful than generic or tokenistic efforts to support LGBT+ staff (Calvard et al., 2019). This was certainly true in my case—those affirming actions had a lasting impact on my sense of belonging.

Llewellyn and Reynolds (2021) emphasise the value of visible LGBT+ networks and explicit allyship demonstrated by leadership to support LGBT+ staff. Upon reflection, both could have been beneficial to me as a trainee teacher. However, since I did not disclose my sexual orientation until my NQT year, such networks and support mechanisms were never presented to me. This underscores a critical point: for support to be genuinely inclusive, it must not depend on disclosure. Networks should be visible and allyship proactive—demonstrated regardless of whether an LGBT+ person is 'known' to be in the room.

A FRESH START

In 2022, I transitioned into a new role as Assistant Headteacher, marking another shift in both setting and professional identity. I was sad to leave a place where I had built such strong relationships, though I was looking forward to the challenge of my new leadership role. Starting at this school was a different experience for me; despite moving before, I was still within the same trust and, therefore, still in regular contact with many of the same colleagues. Part of me was anxious about how to 'come out' again—a common experience for many LGBT+ people—to both colleagues and students. At this point, I made a conscious choice to signify my sexual orientation through visible objects, using LGBT+ pin badges and a pride flag pencil case to purposefully initiate conversations, helping make coming out more organic. While still wanting to usualise my personal identity, I was conscious that doing so required my identity to be known.

When a colleague mentioned that the school had been considering working towards the *Rainbow Flag Award* (a national framework for LGBT+ inclusion in schools, designed by The Proud Trust), I was keen to contribute. This coincided with me starting a Pride Group for students at the school – with student agency and contribution being a key facet of the accreditation. All of this helped me feel more secure in my identity as a gay teacher and a gay leader, through tying elements of my identity as a gay man to more formal elements of my job.

However, this security was not constant. Around seven months in, a new headteacher started at the school. I found myself feeling very anxious in the lead up to him starting, wondering about his attitudes towards LGBT+ inclusion and how this might impact my sense of belonging at work and my inclusion work. It is important to note that he was quick to be very supportive of both.

Though it was not long until I chose to leave this school and return to my previous trust – this time as an Assistant Principal working across its schools – the experiences I had leading LGBT+ inclusion work taught me the importance of engaging more directly in diversity, equality, and inclusion in schools.

BEING A ROLE MODEL

In my own experience, there are powerful benefits to being an LGBT+ role model as a teacher. Stonewall's (2017) report on the experiences of LGBT+ students highlighted how students who know a member of staff who is openly LGBT+ are more likely to feel that there is someone in their school to talk to about being LGBT+. After doing a Pride Month assembly and sharing some of my own experience with students in one of my schools, I was presented with a card and rainbow badge by a Year 11 student I did not know, thanking me for sharing and highlighting that it helped him feel that the school was a place for 'someone like [him]'.

There are also several benefits LGBT+ role models have for the wider student body, such as helping cisgender-heterosexual students to develop their understanding of and empathy towards others (Brett, 2022). Again, this is reinforced through my own experiences, where informal discussions around my personal identity have helped students learn about other experiences (such as the discussion around different forms of marriage with the Year 9 class mentioned earlier).

While being a visible LGBT+ role model can be empowering, there is also the potential of negative pressure and social responsibility when representing a wider group (Calvard et al., 2019; Llewellyn & Reynolds, 2021). This is intensified by the fact that LGBT+ individuals disproportionately experience mental health challenges because of their marginalised identity (Meyer, 2003). As well as impacting on the staff member themselves, there is also the question of how it makes other LGBT+ staff feel. There is the potential that other LGBT+ staff who are not out feel a sense of guilt or pressure where other LGBT+ staff are highlighted as role models (Llewellyn & Reynolds, 2021). For this reason, there should be no expectation that LGBT+ teachers *must* be perceived as role models, whether they are out to students or not. Although, those staff who wish to blend such aspects of their personal identity to enhance their professional identity should not be deterred either, especially where they use this to develop effective inclusion in their setting and usualise the existence of LGBT+ people in day-to-day contexts.

ALLYSHIP FOR INCLUSION

While being an LGBT+ role model is inherently tied to personal identity, the responsibility for fostering inclusion should not fall solely on those who identify as LGBT+; anyone can be an LGBT+ ally. Considering that leaders have significant power to drive effective LGBT+ inclusion (Fletcher, 2022), I would argue that allyship is a position all leaders should adopt. I would also argue that allies in leadership positions hold more power and thus greater potential for supporting the well-being of LGBT+ students and staff. Salter and Migliaccio (2019) found that allies can perpetuate a culture where minority groups are accepted. Given leaders' level of organisational power, they can drive school-level inclusion. For me, the leaders who have explicitly demonstrated allyship—through asking about and listening to my perspective as a gay man, valuing my lived experiences and publicly prioritising LGBT+ issues—have had a significant impact on me feeling able to blend my professional and personal identities, enabling authenticity as both a teacher and a leader.

This necessitates the need for leaders to go beyond reducing discrimination to ensure that LGBT+ staff and students feel safe in school. To be effective allies, leaders must understand what constitutes social safety for LGBT+ staff and students to cultivate inclusive cultures (Brett, 2025). This is certainly mirrored in my own experiences, particularly if I consider the feelings of anxiety I felt when starting at a new school or around the appointment of a new headteacher. In contrast, when leaders have taken the time to speak with me, or other LGBT+ staff and students about our lived experiences, it has promoted a positive sense of self and empowerment. These conversations can help allies to develop a more informed understanding of what it is to be LGBT+, which can lead to more meaningful approaches to supporting LGBT+ inclusion in schools.

REFERENCES

Brassington, J., & Brett, A. (2021). Welcome to Pride & Progress. *Pride & Progress*. Available at: https://podcasts.apple.com/gb/podcast/pride-and-progress/id1560726186

Brett, A. (2022). Under the spotlight: Exploring the challenges and opportunities of being a visible LGBT+ teacher. *Sex Education*, 24(1), 61–75. https://doi.org/10.1080/14681811.2022.2143344

Brett, A. (2025). Safe spaces and beyond: Examining the role of LGBT+ Pride Groups in fostering ontological security and allyship within UK schools. *British Educational Research Journal*. https://doi.org/10.1002/berj.4141

Brett, A., Bodfield, K., Culshaw, A., & Johnson, B. (2024). Exploring LGBTQ+ teacher professional identity through the power threat meaning framework. *British Educational Research Journal*. https://doi.org/10.1002/berj.4060

Brett, A., & Brassington, J. (2023). *Pride & Progress: Making schools LGBT+ inclusive spaces*. Sage.

Butler, J. (1990). *Gender trouble*. Routledge.

Calvard, T., O'Toole, M., & Hardwick, H. (2019). Rainbow lanyards: Bisexuality, queering and the corporatisation of LGBT inclusion. *Work, Employment and Society*, 34(2), 356–368. https://doi.org/10.1177/0950017019865686

Clarke, G. (1996). Conforming and contesting with (a) difference: How lesbian students and teachers manage their identities. *International Studies in Sociology of Education*, 6(2), 191–209. https://doi.org/10.1080/0962021960060

Department for Education. (2011). *Teachers' standards.* Available at: https://www.gov.uk/government/publications/teachers-standards

Endo, H., Reece-Miller, P. C., & Santavicca, N. (2010). Surviving in the trenches: A narrative inquiry into queer teachers' experiences and identity. *Teaching and Teacher Education*, 26(4), 1023–1030. https://doi.org/10.1016/j.tate.2009.10.045

Fenwick, T., & Sanders, S. (2011). Teaching out prejudice–celebrating equality. *Education Review*, 24(1), 61–69.

Fletcher, L. (2022). *Learning from LGBT+ staff across the education sector. Our curriculum needs to be relevant to all young people.* Available at: https://neu.org.uk/latest/library/lgbt-members-survey

Goffman, E. (1959). *The presentation of self in everyday life.* Doubleday.

Khayatt, D. (1997). Sex and the teacher: Should we come out in class? *Harvard Educational Review*, 67(1), 126–144. https://doi.org/10.17763/haer.67.1.27643568766g767m

Khayatt, D., & Iskander, L. (2019). Reflecting on 'coming out' in the classroom. *Teaching Education*, 31(1), 6–16. https://doi.org/10.1080/10476210.2019.1689943

Lee, C. (2019a). How do lesbian, gay and bisexual teachers experience UK rural school communities? *Social Sciences*, 8(9), 249–262. https://doi.org/10.3390/socsci8090249

Lee, C. (2019b). Fifteen years on: The legacy of Section 28 for LGBT+ teachers in English schools. *Sex Education*, 19(6), 675–690. https://doi.org/10.1080/14681811.2019.1585800

- Litton, E. F. (2001). Voices of courage and hope: Gay and lesbian Catholic elementary school teachers. *International Journal of Sexuality and Gender Studies*, 6, 193–205. https://doi.org/10.1023/A:1011538501347

- Llewellyn, A., & Reynolds, K. (2021). Within and between heteronormativity and diversity: Narratives of LGB teachers and coming and being out in schools. *Sex Education*, 21(1), 13–26. https://doi.org/10.1080/14681811.2020.1749040

- Local Government Act. (1988). *Section 28*. Available at: http://www.legislation.gov.uk/ukpga/1988/9/contents

- Meyer, I. H. (2003). Prejudice, social stress, and mental health in lesbian, gay, and bisexual populations: Conceptual issues and research evidence. *Psychological Bulletin*, 129(5), 674–697. https://doi.org/10.1037/0033-2909.129.5.674

- Salter, N. P., & Migliaccio, L. (2019). Allyship as a diversity and inclusion tool in the workplace. *Advanced Series in Management*, 22, 131–152. https://doi.org/10.1108/s1877-636120190000022008

- Stonewall. (2017). *School report: The experiences of lesbian, gay, bi and transgender young people in Britain's schools in 2017*. Available at: https://files.stonewall.org.uk/production/files/the_school_report_2017.pdf?dm=1724230520

- Weems, L. (1999). Pestalozi, perversity, and the pedagogy of love. In W. J. Letts & J. T. Sears (Eds.), *Queering elementary education: Advancing the dialogue about sexualities and schooling* (pp. 27–36). Rowman & Littlefield.

7

LGBTQ+ LEADERSHIP IN THE CATHOLIC SCHOOL CONTEXT

GEORGE WHITE

St Paul's Catholic School, Leicester, UK

Keywords: LGBTQ+ inclusion in faith schools; LGBTQ+ inclusion in religious education; intersectional identities; Catholic teaching; trans Catholic teacher; LGBTQ+ leadership

INTRODUCTION

'Can you be a Catholic and transgender teacher?' This was a question asked directly to me by a student when I first started teaching as Mr White at the Catholic secondary school I attended and was baptised in. I was blindsided. The question necessitated a complex response about what makes a teacher, a Catholic and how those roles can co-exist. Prior to this point, I had not really spoken about my transition at school. During my interview, I was told that I did not need to respond to students' questions about my private life. In hindsight, I wish I had been more open from the outset.

One initial problem with not discussing my transition was the absence of a clear protocol for addressing negative comments. Although such comments were rare, early incidents were mishandled due to the lack of clear behaviour policy and practice. Pupils were neither sanctioned nor educated about appropriate language. This led to a review of the behaviour policy and the development of a new strategy for reporting incidents of hate crimes. This was successfully implemented across our school, and we have seen a reduction in discriminatory comments.

CATHOLIC LEADERSHIP

In Catholic education, there are 'protected positions' that require a 'practising Catholic' to fulfil—typically headteachers, deputies, chaplains and Heads of Religious Education (RE). This, explicitly and implicitly, restricts LGBTQ+ people from applying for or being accepted in these roles. The document *Christ at the Centre* (Catholic Education Service, 2012a) outlines that Catholics who are unable to receive sacraments should be gently declined from these positions. The document goes on to state that you are not a practicing Catholic if you are:

> *...maintaining a partnership of intimacy with another person, outside a form of marriage approved by the Church and which would, at least in the public forum, carry the presumption from their public behaviour of this being a non-chaste relationship.*

Though this applies to all relationships, it is often used to persecute and exclude LGBTQ+ Catholics more forcefully than their heterosexual counterparts.

The official position of the Catholic Church is complex and made up of several documents all with varying degrees of authority for the universal Church as a whole – which lends itself to making this a difficult area to attain leadership with LGBTQ+ content and people in an open dialogue. By exploring the developments in pastoral ministry in support of the LGBTQ+ community during the papacy of Pope Francis between 2013 and 2025, I hope to share insights that allow for leadership in the areas of curriculum, prayer and policy.

LEGAL LANDSCAPE

I am aware that teachers may not know how to discuss LGBTQ+ rights in the context of education, but choosing to remain silent about it does a great disservice to both LGBTQ+ and non-LGBTQ+ people. There is no conflict between church teaching and respecting the human dignity of each person, supporting them pastorally and allowing them to participate fully in community. Learning about our diversity in dignity is one of the ways in which Catholic schools embody a call to love their neighbour and fulfil the teaching above. Under the Equality Act (2010), LGBTQ+ people are protected from discrimination. It is unlawful to victimise or directly or indirectly discriminate i.e., to treat pupils less favourably because of their gender reassignment. The advice for school leaders, school staff, governing bodies and local authorities (DfE, 2014, para 1.8) states:

> *...if a school treats bullying which relates to a protected ground less seriously than other forms of*

> *bullying – for example dismissing complaints of homophobic bullying or failing to protect a transgender pupil against bullying by classmates – then it may be guilty of unlawful discrimination.*

Catholic schools are not exempt from the provisions of the Equality Act. At the time I experienced discriminatory comments, neither I nor the senior leadership team was aware of this legal obligation. I would argue that a comprehensive understanding of equalities legislation is essential for anyone stepping into, or aspiring towards, educational leadership.

However, the legal landscape is complex. Under certain conditions, a difference in treatment may be lawful where a religious or belief organisation excludes individuals of a particular sexual orientation from specific roles, services or activities, or its provision of goods, facilities and services. While this exemption tends to apply more clearly to private bodies than to public institutions, such as government-funded schools, it nonetheless complicates the legal position.

A fuller picture emerges when the Equality Act is read alongside the Human Rights Act of 1998, which protects key freedoms including:

- Article 8: Right to private and family life—this includes a right to identity and personal development, which would include gender reassignment/civil partnerships.

- Article 9: Freedom of thought, conscience and religion.

- Article 10: Freedom of expression.

- Article 14: Prohibition of discrimination.

These rights mean that admissions decisions, for example, cannot lawfully exclude pupils based on the sexual orientation of their parents. School leaders involved in admissions processes should be aware of the following when making judgements on applications for all pupils.

CATHOLIC TEACHING ON LGBTQ+ PEOPLE

The official teaching of the Catholic Church is found in a book titled *The Catechism of the Catholic Church* (Catholic Church, 1994, para. 2358), which states that homosexual persons 'must be accepted with sensitivity, compassion and respect. Any sign of unjust discrimination in their regard should be avoided'. It goes on to state that 'homosexual persons are called to chastity'. There are several documents that I will refer to below which have been produced by the magisterium – the teaching authority of the Catholic Church – which further highlight the position the church takes on LGBTQ+ people, but it is important to note at this stage that the Church often confuses sexuality with gender or talks of the two separately. The acronym 'LGBTQ+' has been used once in the history of Church documentation, and this was in 2023 when collating the information from the Synod.

In April 2024, the Catholic Church released *Dignitas Infinita* (Dicastery for the Doctrine of the Faith, 2024), which reaffirmed the doctrine of previous statements on gender while, for the first time, publicly calling those in the Church to stand up against the criminalisation of people due to their sexual orientation. It states that the Church wishes:

> *...to reaffirm that every person, regardless of sexual orientation, ought to be respected in his or her dignity and treated with consideration, while 'every sign of unjust discrimination' is to be carefully avoided, particularly any form of aggression and violence.*

For this reason, it should be denounced as contrary to human dignity the fact that, in some places, not a few people are imprisoned, tortured and even deprived of the good of life solely because of their sexual orientation. The last section of the letter states that there are:

> ...*violations to the inalienable dignity of humans labelling sex change intervention negatively. At the same time, we are called to protect our humanity, and this means, in the first place, accepting it and respecting it as it was created. It follows that any sex-change intervention, as a rule, risks threatening the unique dignity the person has received from the moment of conception.*

When challenged on this, Pope Francis clarified that the criticism in *Dignitas Infinita* was directed at 'gender ideology' rather than transgender people. In correspondence with Sr Jeannine Gramick (2024), a long-time advocate for LGBTQ+ Catholics, he reaffirmed that 'transgender people must be accepted and integrated into society'. He elaborated that gender ideology 'nullifies differences' and is distinct from the lived realities of trans people, who he described as being deserving of dignity and pastoral care.

SCHOOL LEADERSHIP IN ACTION

From what we have seen in the *Instrumentum Laboris* (General Secretariat of the Synod, 2023), the contributions of LGBTQ+ people have been recorded, visibly—perhaps most obviously included for the first time in the history of the Church. In addition, we as a Church have been asked how to create safe spaces for all those who have been excluded, including LGBTQ+ people, where they instead feel welcome.

Leadership in creating safe spaces must involve facilitating and empowering young people to share their experiences. In his autobiography *Hope*, Pope Francis (2025) explicitly referenced the inclusion of LGBTQ+ people stating, 'everyone in the Church is invited, including people who are divorced, including people who are homosexual, including people who are transgender'. He shared this moment from the first time he formally met with a group of transwomen at his papal audience stating:

> ...*they left in tears, moved because I had taken their hands, had kissed them. As if I had done something exceptional for them. But they are daughters of God! They can receive baptism on the same conditions as other believers and can perform the responsibilities of godparents on the same conditions as others and likewise be witnesses to a marriage. No provision of canonical law forbids it.*

He went on to add that:

> ...*homosexuality is not a crime; it is a human fact. [LGBTQ+ people] are not 'children of a lesser god.' God the Father loves them with the same unconditional love, He loves them as they are, and He accompanies them in the same way that He does with all of us: being close by, merciful, and tender."*

Pope Francis was the leader of the Catholic Church and set an example to those of us in leadership to extend welcome to all people, our policies and procedures should reflect this pastoral approach. In my own experience, I saw this pastoral approach embodied by the headteacher at my first school, a Catholic girls' school in London. Two pupils came out as transgender (female to male), and our headteacher wrote a letter of support which went out to parents. She said that it was within the Catholic values of the school to support these pupils in finding their identity; we were to use their chosen names, and they were permitted a change in uniform. This was wonderful for me to see as someone who had not yet come out as trans. However, Catholic reporters were not happy, and a tirade of abuse came towards the headteacher, the school and the pupils. Leaders in Catholic contexts must be ready to face some heavy situations when discussing LGBTQ+ inclusions.

CURRICULUM, PRAYER AND POLICY

The final area to explore involves the practical implications, but these suggestions must be considered in a nuanced way as the dialogue is between the protected characteristics of religion and belief, sexual orientation and gender reassignment.

In the new Religious Education Directory (Catholic Education Service, 2012b)—which is now in its second year of being introduced in Catholic schools in the United Kingdom—there is the opportunity to explore the life of openly gay priest, Fr Mychal Judge OFM, who lost his life in the events of 9/11. These visible signs help pupils and staff who are LGBTQ+ to know that they are welcome and accepted, as church teaching says that we should be. There are many ways to celebrate and/or remember the LGBTQ+ community throughout the year. For example, we hosted a school mass with the intention of commemorating Transgender Day of Remembrance on November 20th. This is a day where we remember those who have lost their life due to their transgender identity, whether by murder or suicide. We pray for the souls of the departed and pray for an end to the persecution that they may have faced which led to their deaths. We wrote bidding prayers with this in mind and came together to remember this event with trans people and allies in our community.

In addition, you may choose to look at material that goes out in February, which is LGBT History Month. We wrote prayers for our morning registration in which we included the scripture from Psalm 139:14, 'I praise you, for I am fearfully and wonderfully made' (New Revised Standard Version, 1989), and invited the school to pray together for an end to LGBTQ+ persecution around the world. This kind of education helps us to prevent discrimination which might be directed towards the LGBTQ+ community, especially from an unexamined religious perspective.

LEGAL AND LITURGICAL PRACTICES

Another way of exploring the links between the protected characteristics is to assess the legal rights of LGBTQ+ communities and relationships around the world. In the documentary *The Pope Answers* (Disney+, 2023), Pope Francis talks to a non-binary young person and tells them that people who use scripture to tell this person that they are not welcome are infiltrators who take advantage of the Church for their personal passions, for their personal narrowness. As outlined in *Made in God's Image* (Catholic Education Service, 2018), educators should deal with homophobic, biphobic and transphobic (HBT) bullying the same way we do other discriminatory bullying. Our policies should clearly state that these types of behaviours will be treated in the same way as racism, sexism, ableism and misogyny. The Equality

Act is clear that if we do not treat HBT bullying in the same way, then we are guilty of breaking the law.

Some argue that policies (such as those around uniforms, make-up and behaviour) should be gender neutral so that they apply to all students fairly. Leaders creating policies and training staff should be aware that for students in Catholic Secondary Schools, their Relationships and Sex Education (RSE) should cover the concepts of sexual identity, gender identity and sexual orientation (DfE, 2019). It should also teach about discrimination, prejudice and bullying – including and how to respond and the responsibilities to protect victims. The nature and importance of marriage, including the distinctions between marriage in Church teaching (sacramental marriage, civil marriage, civil partnerships and other stable, long-term relationships) should also be explored within secondary RSE. Furthermore, diversity in sexual attraction and developing sexuality, including sources of support and reassurance and how to access them, should be covered (Catholic Education Service, 2019).

In the school resources provided by each diocese for the Synod on Synodality 21–24, pupils are asked the question: *Who are the people who feel excluded and left out of the church?* In my experience, lots of pupils identified the LGBTQ+ community among others. This is a great tool for providing school leaders with an insight into how pupils truly see their educational space and help to facilitate the empowerment of all in your community.

CONCLUSION

Based on my interview with Fr James Martin SJ (Quest, 2022) – who was commended by Pope Francis for his work with LGBTQ+ Catholics—I offer the following reflections for those seeking to lead on LGBTQ+ Inclusion in Catholic schools. Firstly, actively listen to the experiences and stories of LGBTQ+ people and respect the language they use to describe themselves. Where appropriate, and with permission, share their stories or provide space for them to speak directly. Small acts of visibility, such as adding your pronouns to your email signature, signal respect and allyship. Secondly, embrace the Church's call to 'accompaniment'. Leadership means reaching out to those on the peripheries, those who are excluded and to walk with them on their journey. Catholics can celebrate pride month when the focus is on human dignity and preventing unjust discrimination. Similarly, recognising important community, such as Trans Day of Remembrance, can help foster inclusion. Finally, make your commitment to LGBTQ+ people visible. Display materials that affirm LGBTQ+ people of faith, such as the posters created by Stonewall. Integrate inclusive language and imagery into worship, liturgy and everyday interactions. These suggestions are in line with Church teachings which call upon Catholics to accept LGBTQ+ people with compassion, sensitivity and respect. Ultimately, educational leadership in Catholic schools must be about building communities where every person can thrive.

REFERENCES

Catholic Church. (1994). *Catechism of the Catholic church* (2nd ed.). Libreria Editrice Vaticana.

Catholic Education Service. (2012b). *Religious education curriculum directory for Catholic schools and colleges in England and Wales.* https://www.catholiceducation.org.uk/resources/religious-education-curriculum-directory

Catholic Education Service. (2012a). *Christ at the centre: Why the church provides Catholic schools.* https://www.catholiceducation.org.uk/resources/christ-at-the-centre

Catholic Education Service. (2018). *Made in God's image: Challenging homophobic and biphobic bullying in Catholic schools* (2nd ed.). https://www.catholiceducation.org.uk/

Catholic Education Service. (2019). *A model secondary Catholic RSE curriculum.* https://www.catholiceducation.org.uk/resources/model-secondary-catholic-rse

Department for Education. (2014). *The Equality Act 2010 and schools: Departmental advice for school leaders, school staff, governing bodies and local authorities.* https://assets.publishing.service.gov.uk/media/5a7e3237ed915d74e33f0ac9/Equality_Act_Advice_Final.pdf

Department for Education. (2019). *Relationships education, relationships and sex education (RSE) and health education: Statutory guidance for governing bodies, proprietors, head teachers, principals, senior leadership teams, teachers.* https://www.gov.uk/government/publications/relationships-education-relationships-and-sex-education-rse-and-health-education

Dicastery for the Doctrine of the Faith. (2024). *Dignitas Infinita.* Vatican Publishing House.

Disney+. (2023). *The Pope answers.* Disney. [Film].

Francis. (2025). *Hope: The autobiography* (R. Dixon, Trans.) Viking.

Equality Act. (2010). c. 15. *legislation.gov.uk*. https://www.legislation.gov.uk/ukpga/2010/15/contents

General Secretariat of the Synod. (2023). *Instrumentum Laboris: XVI ordinary general assembly of the Synod of Bishops – for a Synodal church: Communion, participation, mission*. Vatican Publishing House. https://www.synod.va/content/dam/synod/common/phases/assembly/Instrumentum-Laboris-ENG.pdf

Gramick, J. (2024, May 1). *After Vatican text, pope tells Jeannine Gramick: Trans people 'must be accepted'*. National Catholic Reporter. https://www.ncronline.org/vatican/vatican-news/after-vatican-text-pope-tells-jeannine-gramick-trans-people-must-be-accepted

New Revised Standard Version. (1989). *The Holy Bible*. National Council of Churches.

Quest. (2022, June 16). *LGBT+ inclusion in Catholic schools: A conversation with Fr James Martin SJ*. YouTube. Video. https://www.youtube.com/watch?v=Oa-l7zTfMyA

8

SAYING YES, SAYING NO: NAVIGATING BEING AN LGBTQ+ LEADER IN SECONDARY SCHOOLS AND FURTHER EDUCATION

JONNY TRIDGELL

University of Oxford, UK

Keywords: LGBTQ+ leadership; LGBTQ+ leadership in secondary education; LGBTQ+ leadership in further education; coming out; queer visibility; teacher identity

INTRODUCTION

There are many ways to be LGBTQ+ in schools. Staff may keep this entirely private (as is their right) or choose to share their identity with only some colleagues or with everyone, including students. This diversity is reflected in LGBTQ+ leadership. Living as ourselves, embodying LGBTQ+ inclusion, is an act of leadership, as is working to queer the curriculum, running a student group or becoming a school's 'go-to' person for all things queer. Through this chapter, I offer guidance to LGBTQ+ colleagues and allies on what it means to be an LGBTQ+ leader and the importance of developing school cultures that allow LGBTQ+ leadership to flourish.

SIR, ARE YOU GAY?

It took me a while to become an LGBTQ+ leader. I have always been open with colleagues but coming out as gay or queer to the wider community was a slow process; it was even longer before I began taking the lead on LGBTQ+ inclusion. There are many reasons for this, including the long shadow of Section 28 of the Local Government Act 1988. Whilst no teacher or school were prosecuted under Section 28, it has been widely shown to have created a climate of fear and a culture of silence that survived its 2003 abolition. It is hard to know how much this slowed my coming out as a teacher (I qualified in 2009, aged 23), though I think it underpinned my worries that being open about my identity was unprofessional and that coming out at school was the same as talking about my sex life. This was shaped by the heteronormative assumption that because heterosexuals did not 'announce' their sexuality (though many teachers openly talk about their opposite-sex partner), it was somehow inappropriate or attention-seeking to be open about mine.

Teaching RE didn't help; both GCSE and A-level courses I taught involved discussing the 'dilemma' of homosexuality, which often resulted in open discussions about whether gay people should form families. The requirement that teachers stay politically neutral (DfE, 2023) had implications, as I worried about being seen as biased, or pushing a nefarious 'agenda' if I were to be open about my sexuality. Now I lean into this—of *course* I have an agenda—I want LGBTQ+ liberation and the end of cisheteronormativity, as should we all. Of course, my fear of homophobic backlash from students and their parents played a crucial role in preventing me being open about my identity.

I had been teaching for around four years when I began saying yes to the question '*sir, are you gay?*', slowly graduating to volunteering this information myself when it felt relevant (though some questions remained firmly unanswered). Before then, my standard response had been '*none of your business*' or '*that's personal*'; it was clear that I wasn't fooling at least some of my students, though there were several who remained oblivious to this, parroting right-wing newspaper diatribes and conspiracy theories about gay people. Simply by being open, and answering the question when it was asked, I became an LGBTQ+ leader—not in the sense of having leadership responsibility *per se* (though by then I had become a head of year), but by being a role model and challenging the status quo. For many educators, this is how they do LGBTQ+ leadership, and this should be praised.

In 2016, I was asked to lead morning assemblies for a week, one year group a day. I enjoy assemblies—embracing my inner show-off—but this felt different. I started by asking students about their favourite and least favourite words or expressions, then shared two particularly egregious phrases: *man up* and *that's so gay*. So far, so normal—a hopefully engaging assembly challenging misogyny and homophobia. What made it different was that I steeled myself, said '*I'm gay*' and explained the impact these phrases had on me, a queer man who does not necessarily conform to gender norms. This signalled a change in my professional identity; I went from being the gay teacher to being the teacher that advocated for and discussed LGBTQ+ rights, cementing my role as the go-to person for LGBTQ+ inclusion. I went on to set up the school's first LGBTQ+ group and began a wider equality, diversity and inclusion journey exploring inclusive curriculum design. It is worth noting that my journey is not uncommon; it mirrors the reality of many LGBTQ+ people who come out at work (Scheadler et al., 2023).

I firmly believe that you do not owe anyone your identity. For most LGBTQ+ people coming out is an iterative process, something we do our whole lives. Personally, I've found it to become easier over time, but I have been fortunate. When I led that assembly, I had worked at the same school for several years, was Head of Sixth Form (so was perhaps more insulated that I would have been as an early career teacher or as a new member of staff) and had a store of credibility and good relationships – all of which provided some cushioning. I say this to reassure you, if you are reading this and feel guilty or worried about coming out, and to encourage empathy if you are working with a colleague who has not said (and may never say) yes to this question. For some, coming out fully at work is not possible; for others it may happen slowly. Not everybody who is LGBTQ+ wants to become a visible LGBTQ+ leader.

Things were not always rosy. I experienced homophobia from students, though this mostly stemmed from students trying to hurt my feelings. The fact that some reached for homophobia as a tool to upset doesn't diminish its cruelty, of course, and shows that homophobia was endemic enough for it to *be* a tool. However, for some homophobia was the cause of their hostility, often validated or encouraged by their parents, which made it difficult to combat. Still, unashamedly saying yes, fully embracing and celebrating my identity, has been unbelievably rewarding. I felt safer at school, no longer second-guessing what I was saying or waiting to be clocked. Living this out loud in my work as a teacher has felt like magic. I have been able to be for many young people the person I needed when I was a boy, showing queer students that they can become queer adults. I have had far more gratitude from students and their parents than I have ever had criticism, even if the criticism has often rung more loudly in my ears. The sweet has generally far outweighed the bitter.

JONNY, CAN I ASK YOU...?

Saying yes to queerness becoming part of my work has given me an additional sense of purpose. I talk about being queer because this is an important part of my positionality, the way I see the world and how I interact with it. Wanda Pillow (2003) writes powerfully about positionality in educational research; much of this rings true, I think, for how we can think about and express our own positionality as teachers. Being out and speaking joyously about LGBTQ+ people and our value has allowed me to have an impact on the lived experience of many people.

By setting up and running my school's first LGBTQ+ group, I was able to provide a safe space for many young people and to be privileged to hear their stories, many of which were as life-affirming and gorgeous as you might hope. In queering my curriculum to include LGBTQ+ people I have helped LGBTQ+ young people feel *seen*. Young (2004) notes that keeping marginalised groups invisible or allowing them only to have visibility through stereotypes or negative representation is central to oppression. This means we need teachers to make LGBTQ+ people and communities visible, in all their complexity, and without falling into the 'kill your gays' trope that considers queer people only through the lens of their oppression and their suffering. Here we need what Sue Sanders, the co-founder of LGBT+ History Month, calls *usualising*, where the presence of LGBTQ+ people in multiple places across the curriculum is entirely normal. As a Lead Practitioner, I was able to discuss ways of including queer people and queer theory across a variety of subjects, whether that meant the occasional use of an LGBTQ+ person in examples (e.g., *'Niamh is thinking about what to get her wife for Christmas…'*), choosing an LGBTQ+ inclusive play in drama, encouraging science teachers to reflect on how they teach about sex and gender, or promoting queer theory as an academic lens (a precise definition of queer theory can be tricky, but it is well worth investigating. Key thinkers include Michel Foucault and Judith Butler, but the concept is understood in many ways by different people!). Witnessing how teachers incorporated LGBTQ+ themes filled me with joy as I saw the important work already being done e.g., modern language displays and lessons on non-binary pronouns.

Becoming a school's go-to person can be extraordinarily empowering. I have been able to spare students and colleagues the labour of having to repeatedly explain their identity; the impact of this on trans and non-binary young people has been starkly shown in research (Bower-Brown et al., 2023). I have guided conversations about school policies and dispelled myths. Leading training on LGBTQ+ inclusion in schools and in higher education has been joyous, marking some of the highlights of my career. Training makes a meaningful difference by providing space for colleagues to discuss their own experiences and ask questions about supporting their students, or, occasionally, their own children.

People are curious, so it is important to set boundaries, even (perhaps *especially*) if you are positioned as an LGBTQ+ leader in schools. Being the go-to person can be emotionally exhausting (see Alcoff, 2022, for insights into extractivism), especially when well-intentioned colleagues might ask overly personal questions (for example about your coming out experience) or ask for your thoughts, without warning, on something terrible that has happened to an LGBTQ+ person in the news or school. It is perfectly acceptable to respond to *'can I ask you about…'* with *'not right now'* or *'no'*. I would encourage anyone who is engaged in LGBTQ+ leadership in school (including those with no additional time or compensation) to share their boundaries with senior leaders and colleagues. For any allies reading this book, please think carefully about how you ask questions and why. Curiosity is, in itself, not a good reason to demand emotional labour of someone, and we must be mindful of this when approaching minoritised people. I have found the concept of *non-extractivism* useful, which recognises that we should not use minoritised people as a source of information alone or in ways that compromise their dignity or wellbeing, even if we feel it will benefit others.

Importantly, a myriad of factors shapes my experience of being LGBTQ+, including my other identities as a white, cisgender, able-bodied, middle-class man. We all experience oppression differently, and it is crucial that LGBTQ+ leaders are not held up either as sole spokespeople, thus contributing to the exclusion of people with different queer experiences, or as infallible oracles and arbiters of what it means to be queer. Leaders must find a balance between protecting marginalised people from unnecessary labour and presuming to speak for others about their experience, a challenge often discussed by Black feminist scholars. Sometimes, this is the difference between saying '*yes*' and '*I'm not sure*', '*I don't know—let me see if I can find out*' or '*you might like to read/watch/listen…*'

Saying yes does carry personal risk, including complaints from parents. One parent complained that I was '*too gay*', and another parent accused our LGBTQ+ club of '*grooming*' her daughter. In both cases, I was defended by the school, though this did not mean these were not distressing experiences. In situations where you do not have SLT backing, it is important to draw on other resources, like those of your teaching union (please make sure you are part of a union, especially one with a strong LGBTQ+ network). By being openly gay and unapologetically promoting LGBTQ+

inclusion, you risk the subtler challenges that can come from parents or students who would prefer you to not *'shove it everyone's face'* or from those who have been fed a toxic diet of transphobia (sometimes masquerading as feminism), misogyny and anti-wokeness by the media. This is, unfortunately, a risk from colleagues, though I have happily encountered only a handful who have actively pushed back against inclusion, sometimes using phrases like *'I think we've gone far enough with this'* or *'I just want to teach them science, not politics'*, though this has included more mendacious accusations, including one colleague who told senior leaders I was attempting to have every child question their gender.

HOW CAN WE HELP LGBTQ+ COLLEAGUES SAY YES?

The challenges facing LGBTQ+ leaders can be dispiriting. I would like, at this point, to reiterate that saying yes—being openly gay and doing LGBTQ+ work in schools—has been one of my greatest joys. This has been made easier by several superb line managers and safeguarding leads who have supported me in this work, whether that be through dealing with homophobic complaints or making space for me to lead assemblies or conduct student voice. My ability to set boundaries has been made possible by others, including LGBTQ+ allies, stepping up to share the labour and because of a strong support network at work and in my personal life. I am very much aware that our society does not afford everyone the same privilege.

How can leaders support colleagues in saying yes? Some of this is about enabling individuals, but so much is about creating a culture where LGBTQ+ leadership is usualised.

Here are some suggestions (and I'd encourage LGBTQ+ colleagues to put these to senior leaders):

- **Pay people for their labour** and provide them additional time to do it. This is simple, but often goes ignored in equalities work. An extra hour's planning time can go a long way!

- **Put LGBTQ+ people in your policies,** including policies around Pride groups, dealing with anti-LGBTQ+ prejudice and how you will ensure that trans+ students and staff can access toilets and other crucial provision.

- **Provide time and funds for proper training.** Costa (2024) has shown training to be more effective if it is done over time and with support for implementation—mandatory one-offs rarely work. This should include explicit training on non-extractive allyship that foregrounds LGBTQ+ people's dignity.

- **Conduct student and staff voice** to understand your school's context and climate, with options for anonymity. Do not blithely assume that the school is inclusive for all LGBTQ+ people.

- **Read!** There are plenty of queer-authored and accessible books available, from *The Transgender Issue* (Faye, 2022) to *Straight Jacket* (Todd, 2016). I recommend *Pride & Progress* (Brett & Brassington, 2023) to all educators.

- **Always model inclusion.** LGBTQ+ people should not have to wait for a disaster to find out that senior leaders are allies. Yes, fly the Progress Flag and put pronouns in email signatures, but don't assume that doing this is enough. Usualise LGBTQ+ people in curricula, talk positively about queer people, proactively use LGBTQ+ inclusive language and avoid falling into exclusionary binaries like gender-specific uniform policies.

- **Listen** when LGBTQ+ leaders say something is hard or difficult or important, even if you do not quite understand why this is the case, and don't demand resilience against oppression.
- **Be grateful.** This is the most important. If someone shares that they are LGBTQ+, recognise this for the honour it is. Say thank you for the emotional labour they perform and remember this if you deliver difficult news of a complaint or ask them for their wisdom.

CONCLUSION

I have sought to show that becoming an LGBTQ+ leader is worth it, despite some of the challenges. To my LGBTQ+ colleagues, know that many of these can be mitigated with good senior leadership support to say yes, and by giving yourself the grace and space to say no when you need to. Whatever form of leadership you embrace, know that your impact will be enormous, even if it does not manifest for some people for months or years to come. School leaders, it is your responsibility to ensure that saying yes need not require courage or a safety net, but that doing so is a cause of celebration. Schools should produce young people who are kind, curious and brave, and this can only happen if everyone is safe to be themselves and make decisions free from fear. LGBTQ+ leadership is a necessary expansion of what teaching can and should be—ethical, inclusive and transformative.

REFERENCES

Alcoff, L. M. (2022). Extractivist epistemologies. *Tapuya: Latin American Science, Technology and Society*, 5(1).

Bower-Brown, S., Zadeh, S., & Jadra, V. (2023). Binary-trans, non-binary and gender-questioning adolescents in UK school. *Journal of LGBT Youth*, *20*(1), 1–18.

Brett, A., & Brassington, J. (2023). *Pride & Progress, making schools LGBTQ+ inclusive spaces*. Sage Publications.

Costa, E. (2024). Examining the effectiveness of interventions to reduce discriminatory behaviour at work: An attitude dimension consistency perspective. *Journal of Applied Psychology*, *109*(2), 245–259.

Department for Education. (2023). *Guidance: Political impartiality in schools*. https://www.gov.uk/government/publications/political-impartiality-in-schools/political-impartiality-in-schools

Faye, S. (2022). *The transgender issue: An argument for justice*. Penguin Books.

hooks, b. (1989). Choosing the margin as a space of radical openness. *The Journal of Cinema and Media*, *36*.

Pillow, W. (2003). Confession, catharsis, or cure? Rethinking the uses of reflexivity as methodological power in qualitative research. *International Journal of Qualitative Studies in Education*, *16*(2), 175–196. https://doi.org/10.1080/0951839032000060635

Sanders, S. (2021). Visualising and usualising the LGBTQ+ community. *TED Talks*. [Video]. https://www.ted.com/talks/sue_sanders_visibilising_and_usualising_the_lgbtq_community

Scheadler, T. R., Haus, K. R., Mobley, T. A., & Mark, K. P. (2023). LGBTQ+ grassroots activism: An opportunity for resilience. *Journal of Homosexuality*, *70*(3), 347–365.

Todd, M. (2016). *Straight Jacket: Overcoming society's legacy of gay shame*. Bantam Press.

Young, I. (2004). Five faces of oppression. In L. M. Heldke & P. O'Connor (eds), *Oppression, privilege & resistance: Theoretical perspectives on racism, sexism and heterosexism* (pp. 37–63). McGraw-Hill.

9

HOPE THROUGH SUPPORTIVE AND CHALLENGING SCHOOL GOVERNANCE

GARY PYKITT

Birmingham City University, UK

Keywords: LGBTQ+ governance; critical pedagogy in governance; LGBTQ+ representation in schools; critical consciousness in education; inclusive governing bodies; LGBTQ+ safeguarding in schools

INTRODUCTION

Amid the pressures of neoliberal accountability, schools are faced with various competing priorities. As volunteers, governors play a significant role in the strategic oversight and decision-making of schools, shaping vision, ethos and direction. Being a governor is a privilege, and it is incredibly rewarding, but it also comes with significant responsibility. This includes supporting the school's strategic direction through policy development, holding leaders accountable for performance and attendance, ensuring a balanced curriculum and maintaining robust safeguarding policies and procedures. Overseeing financial performance and ensuring responsible use of funds also fall under the governors' remit. All of this must be carried out in the school's and stakeholders' best interests with probity, fairness and transparency.

With so many responsibilities, it is probably unsurprising that LGBT+ inclusivity and representation can be overlooked or deprioritised. Leaders' and teachers' personal and professional uncertainties around LGBT+ inclusion—often exacerbated by fears of negative parental reactions—can cause confusion and concern about what they are and are not 'allowed' to do. This is often intensified by the media and wider socio-political context. As Forrest (as cited in Cole, 2018, p. 135) observes in relation to the 2017 review of the sex and relationships curriculum, 'organisations arguing that it will corrupt children's innocence can still find an airing in the media despite no evidence supporting the claim'.

Drawing on critical pedagogy and theories of hope, this chapter explores how governance can play a pivotal role in securing meaningful and impactful change. A broad skillset is needed on a governing board, and there is a need to focus on how governance can 'build more hopeful and just futures' (Morley et al., 2020, p. 12) through investment and perseverance. The path may not be straightforward, but this chapter considers how governors can persevere to support good outcomes for all.

A CRITICAL PEDAGOGY APPROACH TO INCLUSIVE GOVERNANCE

Critical Pedagogy, according to Giroux (2020, p. 179) is about questioning 'common sense' assumptions and thus seeking alternative possibilities. Seal and Smith (2021, p. 1) highlight that critical pedagogy, 'goes right to the heart of what education is about, who it is for and how it is done'. It is about awareness of, and learning from the lived experiences of others, thinking critically with principles of democracy, equity and diversity at heart. This can be challenging, and hope is needed to be able to effect change and take positive action as part of a critical pedagogical approach. Freire (1992, p. 2) emphasises the importance of capitalising on opportunities for hope, regardless of potential barriers, as passivity and apathy result in 'hopelessness and despair'. Active consideration of LGBT+ inclusivity and representation may not be on governors' radar and is often avoided due to its controversial and contentious portrayal in public discourse (Hamilton, 2021), despite progress in legislation and policy. Forrest (as cited in Cole, 2018, pp. 164–165) highlights that 'fear of the censure that might come from the press and concerns about parental views leads to some self-censuring'. While there needs to be awareness of the potential for negative responses, Boyd and Roper note (as cited in Maude & Davies, 2025, pp. 106–107) that the requirement for schools, through *Relationships and Sex Education* (DfE, 2025a), to teach about varying family types, including LGBT+,

> *...has raised some concern from parents; however, the DfE sees value in this early introduction in a drive to promote a sense of tolerance and respect to help counter the increasing amount of homophobia that is present in the media.*

AN UNHELPFUL HISTORICAL LEGACY

There is a long history of negative connotations around the concept of homosexuality, which continues today. Foucault (1979, p. 43) reminds us that, 'We must not forget that the psychological, psychiatric, medical category of homosexuality was constituted from the moment it was characterised'. The vague wording of Section 28 has a continuing legacy, as noted by Lee (2019) who found that LGBT teachers who experienced Section 28 remain extremely cautious, vigilant and anxious in their school workplaces. It is important that we take account of the impact of Section 28 on all stakeholders, including those who were teaching and those being educated under Section 28 (1988–2003). Brett and Brassington (2023, p. 7) emphasise the importance of visibility and respect for LGBT+ identities stating, 'Section 28 meant that LGBT+ young people had to grow up in a culture of silence and fear, without role models or someone to turn to'. This backdrop is important for governors to be aware of as it will impact the pace of progress. Unhelpful myths about 'promoting' homosexuality still exist today. Ferfolja and Ullman (2020, p. 53) note the misconceptions perpetrated around LGBT+ inclusive education, such as 'teaching *how* to be 'homosexual' rather than teaching *about* related issues and identities'.

GOVERNOR RESPONSIBILITIES

Governing boards have specific safeguarding responsibilities. The Department for Education (DfE, 2025b, p. 8) states that as part of the systems to support safeguarding in schools, there should be a 'behaviour policy (which should include measures to prevent cyberbullying, prejudice-based and discriminatory bullying)'. It also states the duty of governing boards in relation to the Equality Act (2010) and the Public Sector Equality Duty (PSED) to 'carefully consider how they are supporting their pupils...with regard to particular protected characteristics – including disability, sex, sexual orientation, gender reassignment and race' (DfE, 2024, p. 27). It is important to remember that governance, which is both supportive and challenging, can provide hope for meaningful representation and inclusivity of LGBT+ identities in all schools.

Governors should work together, not just agreeing decisions but supporting and challenging one another to ensure accountability and that their focus remains strategic. Being strategic relates to the longer-term picture, considering the vision and goals as well as ratifying key documents, including policies. A governor's role is to scrutinise and approve policies written by school leaders and to hold leaders to account for their effective implementation. The line between strategic and operational is not always clearcut but oversight and scrutiny are the hallmarks of governance; being curious, inquisitive and probing. Governors, to make decisions based on the best interests of children, should not just merely rubber stamp policies. While all schools may not have a specific LGBT+ Policy, the Diversity, Equity and Inclusivity Policy (or equivalent) will be key as will other policies in terms of how they embed LGBT+ representation throughout all aspects of the school's work.

Governor monitoring is essential to provide assurance that policy is translating into practice so the impact can be reviewed and feed into future policy development. Governor visits to school are essential to understand, support and challenge the implementation and impact of policy to promote ongoing reflection and reflexivity to enable development. Barnes and Carlile (2018, p. 37) emphasise that, 'School policies...do not prove that an institution is actually doing something'. Barnes and Carlile (2018) also note the importance of naming every protected characteristic from the Equality Act so that there is a clear and visible commitment to treating everyone with equality and fairness. Governors should read policies with criticality and consider if they:

- Reflect the vision, values, inclusive ethos and culture of the school.
- Take account of different forms of bullying, how it may affect specific groups and actions to mitigate risks.
- Clearly relate to each named protected characteristic.
- Show an initiative-taking approach.
- Clearly state the action that will be taken to implement the policy and the process for monitoring the impact.
- Clearly show the involvement of all stakeholders.
- Show how they relate to other aspects of the school's work.
- Include the monitoring of a range of activity, including elicitation of staff, pupil and parent/carer voice.
- Are clear for all stakeholders to understand.
- Are informed by research that reflects current data, thinking and debates.
- Meet the specific context of the school.
- Encourage tailored provision for specific needs through the principle of equity.
- Show awareness of the dangers of making 'heterosexual assumptions' which can marginalise and stigmatise LGBT+ identities (Forrest, as cited in Cole, 2018, p. 167).

GOVERNOR KNOWLEDGE, SKILLS AND UNDERSTANDING

In today's rapidly evolving information landscape, governors must remain critically aware of misinformation, disinformation and polarised debates. Social media and the rapid growth of AI means that polarised views have the potential to spread quickly with little foundation in fact or critically balanced understanding. The diversity within individual governing boards has been a matter of consternation for some time and is stubbornly tricky to resolve. Age, gender and ethnicity are commonly referenced factors when looking at the constitution of a governing board, yet sexuality and gender diversity are rarely, if ever, mentioned. This could be a result of what Lee (2023, p. 225) describes as, 'the substantial energy and caution (which is) required to navigate the hetero- and cis-normative school community'. Gender categorisation tends to relate to male/female binaries, and the balance of these on the board. The importance of governing boards reflecting their school communities is often emphasised, often from an ethnicity perspective. This is important but governors also need to reflect societal diversity more widely to bring broader perspectives to the table. Despite the challenges of recruiting sufficient governors with the required knowledge, skills and understanding to support the effective running of a board, it remains important to ensure the board is representative of the full range of protected characteristics so that there is opportunity and visibility for diverse voices.

How does the governing board reflect the diversity of family make-ups, including those with same-sex parents? What about non-conformity to traditional gender binaries and stereotypes? If the board is homogenous in its constitution, we run the risk of restricting inclusivity in our thinking and not exploring issues due to a lack of awareness.

Brett and Brassington (2023, p. 87) assert that, 'The first step in getting leadership teams to understand the importance of LGBT+ inclusion is getting them to recognise there is a problem'. In seeking the best opportunities for all children, Back (2020, p. 2) notes that, 'Developing a hopeful understanding must never look away from the trouble'. An example of 'trouble' in the context of governors is ensuring that LGBT+ inclusivity and representation remain on the agenda. The imperative for this is evident in a recent report from the LGBT+ charity, Just Like Us (2024), which found that 48% of lesbian and gay parents worry their child will be bullied because of their family structure. Hope, while a powerful force, must be critically informed. It should not obscure difficult realities. Back (2020, p. 5) draws attention to the work of Lear (2006) on 'worldly radical hope', which 'is cultivated and shaped in the here-and-now by the practice of attentive witnessing, taking in what is happening, interpreting its meaning and the possible gifts to the future that might emerge'. Governors, therefore, must ground their hope in action, critical reflection and a willingness to confront uncomfortable truths.

CRITICAL CONSCIOUSNESS IN ACTION

Governors need to be aware of issues around sexuality and gender in the news and critically engage with the debates, drawing on wider reading and people's personal experience to make informed decisions. Governors who identify as LGBT+ can help to bring this perspective to the table. Diversity in all its forms when reviewing the constitution of the governing board need to be a key consideration, thinking carefully about the insights such variety can bring. There must be a preparedness to have discussions and question assumptions, stereotypes and prejudices so that governors remain open to varying perspectives, so that they can be an ally and advocate for all stakeholders. This may relate to staff who identify as LGBT+, gender questioning children, or those with same-sex parents.

Being a supportive, yet challenging governor will include patience, learning, innovation and problem-solving in order to find appropriate ways forward. Phillips (2024) talks about the importance of governor humility and the willingness to acknowledge gaps in knowledge, understanding or experience. Here we can see the principles of critical pedagogy apply to the work of governors, as Giroux (2020, p. 179) emphasises based on the work of Freire (1970),

> *...it was about offering a way of thinking beyond the seeming naturalness or inevitability of the current state of things, challenging assumptions validated by 'common sense', soaring beyond the immediate concerns of one's experiences, entering into a critical dialogue with history, and imagining a future that would not merely reproduce the present.*

When reviewing and ratifying policies, and visiting schools, governors should consider how students' learning, knowledge, skills and understanding develop through critical engagement, dialogue and the challenging of ideas to support their development as respectful, responsible, and empathetic citizens who are able and confident to challenge injustice. This has the potential to support progress towards a more accepting, inclusive and respectful future for all. A range of knowledge and broad skillset on a governing board will strengthen the critical consciousness required to effect impactful and longer-lasting sustainable change. Seal and Smith (2021, p. 8) outline Freire's three levels of consciousness:

- *Intransitive: People accept the status quo and feel they lack the power/control to bring about change.*

- *Semi-Transitive: There is a sense of understanding, but the issues are seen as inescapable or predetermined. This said, there may be small-scale actions to support change in a confined area.*

- *Critical – 'They see the structural dimensions of their problems, making connections between their problems and the social context in which their problems are embedded, both in terms of analysis and actions that will change their structural oppressions as well as addressing some of their immediate concerns'.*

These notions are complex and nuanced. Governors must continually strive towards the critical level, centring safety, wellbeing and belonging to bring about sustainable and transformational change within their school context and beyond. The governing board should engage with stakeholders to support the fulfilling of their statutory functions (DfE, 2024). When talking to children and their parents/carers, one of the key things to be assured about is if the children (and their families) feel happy and safe in school. As Just Like Us (2024, p. 5) reminds us, 'Lesbian, gay, and trans parents in particular are concerned their children's schools will not be accepting of their LGBT+ family'.

CONCLUSION

Through their role in shaping school vision and ethos – focused on the progress, achievement and wellbeing of all stakeholders – governors have tremendous potential to make an impact on LGBT+ representation, inclusivity and visibility.

As Forrest (in Cole, 2018, p. 184) cites Redman (1994), 'sexuality is "everywhere and nowhere" in school'—an apt description of the silent pervasiveness of heteronormativity. Governors need to ensure there is a clear rationale for LGBT+ inclusivity work in school that is fully integrated in policy and practice, establishing a fully inclusive ethos for all stakeholders. It is not always easy but bringing together a diverse range of stakeholders will help. This said, the people and their knowledge, skills and understanding will not always be enough. Hope is essential to bring about positive outcomes and change. As Freire (1992, p. 2) asserts, 'We need critical hope the way a fish needs unpolluted water'. As school governors, we can ensure hope through our practice by keeping these complex, nuanced issues on the agenda and engaging in meaningful conversation. We need to feel comfortable with the discomfort of not always having a definite answer and seek to know more to ensure the strategic decisions and actions taken benefit all stakeholders within the school.

REFERENCES

Back, L. (2020). Hope's work. *Antipode*, *53*(1), 3–20. https://doi.org/10.1111/anti.12644

Barnes, E., & Carlile, A. (2018). *How to transform your school into an LGBT+ friendly place*. Jessica Kingsley Publishers.

Brett, A., & Brassington, J. (2023). *Pride & Progress*. Corwin.

Charlesworth, J. (2015). *That's so gay! Challenging homophobic bullying*. Jessica Kingsley Publishers.

Cole, M. (Ed.). (2018). *Education, equality and human rights* (5th ed.). Routledge.

Department for Education. (2024). *Maintained schools governance guide.* https://www.gov.uk/guidance/governance-in-maintained-schools

Department for Education. (2025a). *Relationships education, relationships and sex education (RSE) and health education.* https://www.gov.uk/government/publications/relationships-education-relationships-and-sex-education-rse-and-health-education

Department for Education. (2025b). *Keeping children safe in education.* https://www.gov.uk/government/publications/keeping-children-safe-in-education–2

Ferfolja, T., & Ullman, J. (2020). *Gender and sexuality diversity in a culture of limitation.* Routledge.

Foucault, M. (1979). *The history of sexuality: Volume 1—The will to knowledge* (R. Hurley, Trans.). Penguin.

Freire, P. (1970). *Pedagogy of the oppressed.* Penguin.

Freire, P. (1992). *Pedagogy of hope: Reliving pedagogy of the oppressed.* Bloomsbury Academic.

Giroux, H. A. (2020). *On critical pedagogy* (2nd ed.). Bloomsbury Academic.

Hamilton, P. (2021). *Diversity and marginalisation in childhood.* Sage.

Just Like Us. (2024). *LGBT+ parents report.* https://www.justlikeus.org/wp-content/uploads/2024/06/LGBT-parents-report-2024-by-Just-Like-Us.pdf

Lear, J. (2006). *Radical hope: Ethics in the face of cultural devastation.* Harvard University Press.

Lee, C. (2019). Fifteen years on: The legacy of Section 28 for LGBT+ teachers in English schools. *Sex Education*, *19*(6), 675–690. https://doi.org/10.1080/14681811.2019.1585800

Lee, C. (2023). *Pretended: Schools and Section 28*. John Catt.

Local Government Act. (1988). *c. 9, § 28*. https://www.legislation.gov.uk/ukpga/1988/9/section/28/enacted

Maude, K., & Davies, L. (2025). Learning matters. *Diversity, Equity, Inclusion and Teaching*.

Morley, C., Ablett, P., Noble, C., & Cowden, S. (Eds.). (2020). *The Routledge handbook of critical pedagogies for social work*. Taylor & Francis.

Phillips, I. (2024). *How to be a great GoaT*. Brown Dog Books.

Redman, P. (1994). Shifting ground: Rethinking sexuality education. In D. Epstein (Ed.), *Challenging lesbian and gay inequalities in education*. Open University Press.

Seal, M., & Smith, A. (2021). *Enabling critical pedagogy in higher education*. Critical Publishing.

Section 3

REIMAGINING LGBTQ+ LEADERSHIP: HIGHER EDUCATION AND PROFESSIONAL DEVELOPMENT

10

THE JOURNEY OF A LGBTQ+ EDUCATOR, RESEARCHER AND ACTIVIST

ALEX BAIRD

University of Bedfordshire, UK

Keywords: LGBTQ+ leadership in education; trans non-binary educator; diversity, equality, and inclusion (DEI); queer representation in academia; LGBTQ+ teacher experiences UK; inclusive physical education

INTRODUCTION

The AIDS epidemic of the 1980s significantly hindered legal progress and adversely affected public attitudes towards the LGBTQ+ community in the United Kingdom (Clements & Field, 2014). During this time, the introduction of Section 28 legislation (Local Government Act, 1988) led schools to avoid discussing homosexuality altogether. When I attended school from 1985 to 1999, the only sexual orientation addressed was heterosexuality, although I frequently heard homophobic remarks. I was aware of one gay teacher at my secondary school because the other pupils gossiped about her. I recall a moment when a group of girls mocked this teacher behind her back for being seen walking to the staff party with her girlfriend. I challenged them, expressing how brave I thought she was for doing that. At the time, I felt scared that my peers might assume I was gay based on my response, but they did not seem to make that link. Though I admired the teacher's courage and other LGBTQ+ individuals through my involvement in sports outside of school, I now feel saddened that I viewed their actions as requiring bravery. Throughout this chapter, I retrace and reflect upon my journey in the education sector as both a learner and a practitioner, explaining how these experiences have shaped my understanding and approach to leadership. As Frangeskou (2025) also describes, education influenced my decision to go back into the closet and later come out.

UNIVERSITY STUDENT AND TEACHING CAREER

When I arrived at university to pursue a degree in Sports Science and Physical Education, I was concerned that being a hockey player who aspired to become a Physical Education teacher, while also being gay, might come across as cliché. In truth, I knew I was different, but I had not (or I had not been allowed) to accept myself fully. I had been taught that my sexuality was something that should remain unspoken, yet I was following a path that could lead others to stereotype me as gay. I feared facing rejection and hostility and at the time, I did not believe I had the strength to handle or contest any repercussions. Once I began my Post Graduate Certificate in Education, I hoped to connect with LGBTQ+ friends on my course. Although I did find some, and we supported each other, we never discussed the fears and challenges we faced as LGBTQ+ trainee teachers. I never dismissed the notion of becoming a teacher, but I felt compelled to conceal my identity around colleagues and pupils to protect my career prospects. I was aware of the discrimination that I might face teaching, and I certainly did not have the privilege of being open early on in my career when I had little financial security or an established reputation to fall back on. Over the next 13 years, I worked in various schools. In some environments, I felt safer than in others. I came out to a few trusted colleagues in a couple of schools, but I never felt comfortable enough to be open with pupils. I regret this decision, but senior management never provided enough support to take that risk. Looking back, I wish I had used certain incidents in school as 'teaching moments' to address fears and misconceptions, rather than shutting them down defensively.

Physical education is highly gendered; there are long-standing gender inequalities in its policy and practice and physical educators have been slow in responding to and confronting these inequalities (Penney, 2002). I felt more comfortable teaching in mixed-sexed school settings, although I also faced sexism and homophobia in these environments, particularly when seeking promotion. Initially, I focused on the 'what' (knowledge) rather than the 'how' (approach) of my teaching, which was probably a reflection of my competitive sports background and my perfectionism. As I became more adept at addressing the primary challenges of teaching, I grew increasingly critical of the messages I conveyed. I began to challenge male hegemony, gendered stereotypes and heteronormativity within the curriculum, the school setting and extracurricular programmes. Questioning deeply held beliefs in others was a slow process and often led to conflict. Fortunately, I had the support of an experienced group of colleagues during my first middle management position in school. Reflecting now on how I approached this role, I realise that I often relied solely on myself. I had become so accustomed to being self-sufficient and proving my worth to others—traits that can be valuable in life but are not particularly helpful in leadership.

LEAVING SCHOOL TEACHING FOR ACADEMIA

I am proud of my accomplishments in primary and secondary schools, but a series of events left me frustrated and exhausted, ultimately leading me to leave my teaching career. I made every effort to support the education and well-being of the young people I taught. In striving for perfection—partly to protect myself against potential backlash regarding my sexuality (Lee, 2022)—I compromised my own identity to fit into the heteronormative structure. Lecturing in higher education (HE) seemed the next logical step and direction for my career. I felt relieved at the prospect of this move, knowing there would be no backlash from parents. However, this transition proved a shock; I had significantly underestimated the challenges. I had to learn new operational structures, cultures and working practices. At times, my personal and professional values were challenged, and I felt that my experience was undervalued. This left me feeling as though I was contributing very little.

In 2020, the LGBTQ+ staff network was established at the university, and I joined immediately. I met with other LGBTQ+ staff and felt stronger, but I also needed this support as I became more visibly LGBTQ+ to others in the workplace. At this time, as I struggled to navigate my new working culture and experienced a painful loss of my previous teacher identity, I took on a voluntary primary school governor role to maintain some involvement in the school context. As a governor, I became involved in supporting the new statutory Relationships, Sex, and Health Education curriculum (RSHE), specifically the content surrounding 'LGBT families'. This role led to my first piece of research on LGBTQ+ themes. I was not 'out' in the school and, as evidenced by interviewee responses and broader interactions, was not read by others as LGBTQ+. I felt uncertain about the potential consequences of becoming openly LGBTQ+ in the school. I worried that this might restrict my involvement in the school's RSHE curriculum and hinder access to carry out the research. I believe these fears were justified and the backlash I received from undertaking the research confirmed my fears of putting myself out there.

Carrying out the research took an emotional toll on me, particularly with COVID-19 measures in place, which left me relatively isolated when receiving anti-LGBTQ+ emails from parents and hearing misplaced concerns from other governors. Not being 'out' probably led to me hearing more overt homophobia and transphobia, but I mainly doubted my decision when it came to disseminating my research to the school. Perhaps, if I had been visibly LGBTQ+, it might have encouraged the head teacher to allow me to share my research findings with school staff. I took solace from sharing some of my experiences with members of the newly formed LGBTQ+ staff network at my university and organising online panel presentations, which attracted a broader public audience to alleviate misconceptions of RSHE and offer guidance. I began to appreciate my greater agency and autonomy, as well as the opportunities within my new workplace to be authentic and innovative.

REFLECTING ON LGBTQ+ LEADERSHIP

After a year of learning how an LGBTQ+ staff network operates as committee secretary, I was encouraged to become vice chair. I enjoy the position, mainly because I am not the figurehead, allowing me the angle and space to further challenge inequalities within the university. It is also a reflection of how we recognise our strengths and divide duties between the chair and myself. Becoming the sole acting chair of the network for a period of time, heightened my obligation to nurture relationships between the network and the wider university. Being actively involved in the vital work of the LGBTQ+ staff network gave me both the confidence (coming from a growing expertise) and impetus (being fully aware of the problems that needed to be resolved) to put myself forward for the university-wide Diversity, Equality, and Inclusion (DEI) role. This DEI secondment role made me more familiar with university structures, practices, and staff. The secondment also entailed navigating the repercussions of being a hyper-visible LGBTQ+ person in the university. During this time, I came out to others as trans non-binary. Fortunately, my doctoral research involved participating in a LGBTQ+ leadership development programme in UK HE. It allowed me to meet and speak with other LGBTQ+ leaders and mentors. I gained new LGBTQ+ friends. I started to connect the value of my LGBTQ+ lived experiences with my leadership and particularly my sensitivity, a facet that others have often viewed as a weakness. My understanding of leadership has shifted; I now view it as relational and collective. Leadership can also be egalitarian, creative, and transformative. I began to realise that leadership can be enacted at any level within an organisation, rather than requiring an authority role. Though I did not hold any positional power, I was still positively influencing others by drawing upon my personal power. In the DEI aspect of my working role, I began to draw strength from my knowledge and credibility; someone who is able to bring people together, facilitate discussions, navigate tensions, and accelerate creative actions.

LGBTQ+ programme attendees (and participants in my doctoral research) came to the same conclusion about the distinctiveness and potential of LGBTQ+ leadership as programme mentors secured and modelled the association between their LGBTQ+ lives and leadership. LGBTQ+ leadership was seen and enacted as listening to, valuing and developing people and challenging inequalities by voicing an alternative perspective. LGBTQ+ mentorship facilitated intergenerational queer knowledge sharing amongst LGBTQ+ staff in professional services and academic positions. The collective energy of programme attendees coming together readdressed feelings of powerlessness in the university and nurtured and developed LGBTQ+ staff talent. I have established a Diverse Networks of HE group engaging with staff at 30+ universities online to offer support to members and facilitate collaborative projects. I am currently co-designing and guiding two further LGBTQ+ leadership development programmes and I hope my accompanying research will amplify attendees' voices, inspire LGBTQ+ leaders, engage allies, and secure future funding for these programmes.

I found the literature (Ahmed, 2006, 2012; Gino, 2018; Guyan, 2022; Morley & Leyton, 2023; Syed, 2019) I read for my doctorate very useful, particularly when grappling with the internal and external pressures of carrying out the DEI role. I experienced something Sara Ahmed calls a 'brick wall' (a metaphor for coming up against resistance that stops an institution at any level from moving forward). This obstacle might not always be visible to everyone. I have tried to remain calm and compassionate to diffuse conflicts and to strike an appropriate balance between persistence and patience in tackling barriers. I have watched talented people around me and found vital mentors. They have always been encouraging and optimistic about my efforts. They have reminded me to pause, take a step back and acknowledge small wins. I now realise that being vulnerable is a necessary part of the role. The role requires me to draw upon and (at appropriate times) share my own lived experiences and feelings. It entails a responsibility and a willingness to speak up and stand up or make space for others. I experience a deep visceral pain when hearing an apathetic response or worst still, the same arguments repeated against the trans community that have been previously voiced towards the gay community, namely that we are a threat, dangerous predators and groomers, who should hide our identity, at least in public. Still, I have also become more resilient by setting personal boundaries, stepping back when I need to rest and reaching out to allies for support.

INFLUENCING POSITIVE CHANGE

Despite the 2010 Equality Act (which applies to education and employment), I would highlight that gender critical voices in HE, the culture war and moral panic towards trans people constructed by politicians and the media are making HE and wider society less safe for LGBTQ+ and particularly for trans and non-binary people. Sometimes, it feels like we are going backwards. Cisgender voices are the ones making judgements and forming misconceptions about trans people. It is more than rhetoric, though; I know from personal experience obtaining gender-affirming care, securing a legal name change and accessing education, sports and general health care are becoming increasingly intrusive and difficult for trans and non-binary people. The HE sector's precarious financial situation further restricts necessary resources supporting DEI actions. LGBTQ+ organisations facing an increasing demand for their critical work in an already difficult economic climate are being attacked and consequently facing defunding, obstructing them from providing these much-needed services (Walker, 2025). However, there is also a sense of hope from an older generation of LGBTQ+ people who have overcome hostility in the past, along with generations of LGBTQ+ people and their allies who will not allow hard-won positive changes to be easily overturned. I spoke as a delegate in support of the trans healthcare motion at the Trade Union Conference. It was a powerful experience and reminded me of the importance of collective voices coming together to urge a new political party to take positive action.

I want to speak calmly, powerfully and articulately so that I am heard. My viewpoint is sometimes trivialised, even when I know that something significant is happening. I have faced aggressive responses from those who mistakenly pit women's rights against trans rights. Over time, I have grown stronger. I am learning to identify which discussions are worth pursuing and which battles are not worth engaging in. I carefully consider my language to ensure that I communicate effectively with others. I have found that framing a concise statement or a question can be quite persuasive. As I share my experiences, I have noticed the small changes I have made in others, which has boosted my confidence in expressing myself. I try to lead with a strong sense of integrity, compassion, intuition and purpose and these values are shaping my working relationships with others.

I have found a way to build connections between my university teaching, my DEI roles and my research, all of which contribute to addressing inequalities. In the pedagogy units that I lead, I engage students in discussions about social justice, fostering an environment that encourages critical awareness and responsive approaches. I have actively participated in DEI initiatives, including work on committees and events, where I share my expertise with colleagues, senior leaders and community partners. Guided by the university's values and strategies, as well as staff and student data, charter processes and stakeholder input, we have pinpointed issues and begun to transform the university culture. Our goal is to enhance experiences for all individuals, including those from minority groups. My research focuses on LGBTQ+ themes, and I carefully consider how to maximise its impact. This includes identifying potential audiences to share my research with across the UK higher education sector, academia, the corporate sector, the public sector, voluntary organisations, charities and society. I actively seek opportunities to collaborate and integrate the expertise of others. I attend and co-convene relevant events to connect with policymakers, practitioners and stakeholders. Lastly, I track and evaluate these activities to reflect on how I can achieve a more significant impact.

Thankfully, I have found a vital network of other LGBTQ+ researchers and activists who provide me with support, inspiration and solidarity. I will continue to highlight and address important issues. I will continue to seek out allies and look ahead for myself, my community and other marginalised groups to reimagine and create a more inclusive future for us all. I reflect critically on my lived experiences, recognising their value for leadership as I prioritise my purposes and values. I have given myself the time, space and care to know myself better. I know my strengths (my sensitivity, reflexivity, compassion, creativity, determination and queerness) and the structure of the sector in which I work. I feel more self-aware, grounded and connected with others. I am ready to show up and lead with my whole self.

REFERENCES

Ahmed, S. (2006). *Queer phenomenology: Orientations, objects, others*. Duke University Press.

Ahmed, S. (2012). *On being included: Racism and diversity in institutional life*. Duke University Press.

Clements, B., & Field, C. D. (2014). Public opinion toward homosexuality and gay rights in Great Britain. *Public Opinion Quarterly*, 78(2), 523–547.

Frangeskou, F. (2025). Am I an activist? In A. Brett & C. Lee (Eds.), *The guide to LGBTQ+ research*. Emerald Publishing.

Gino, F. (2018). *Rebel talent: Why it pays to break the rules at work and in life*. (Pan Books).

Guyan, K. (2022). *Queer data: Using gender, sex and sexuality data for action*. Bloomsbury Academic.

Lee, C. (2022). How does openness about sexual and gender identities influence self-perceptions of teacher leader authenticity? *Educational Management Administration & Leadership*, 50(1), 140–162.

Local Government Act. (1988). *Section 28*. Available at: www.legislation.gov.uk/ukpga/1988/9/section/28/enacted. Accessed January 11, 2024

Morley, L., & Leyton, D. (2023). *Queering higher education: Troubling norms in the global knowledge economy*. Routledge.

Penney, D. (2002). *Gender and physical education: Contemporary issues and future directions*. Routledge.

Syed, M. (2019). *The power of thinking differently: Rebel ideas*. John Murray.

Walker, C. (2025). *The LGBT+ fund report: The UK LGBT+ voluntary & community sector finances, funding & future*. Available at: www.consortium.lgbt/2025/03/27/new-data-shows-uk-lgbt-organisations-receive-just-10p-in-every-100-of-voluntary-sector-income/

11

THE QUEERED EQUILIBRIUM: REFRAMING LEADERSHIP AND POWER FOR EARLY-CAREER ACADEMICS

CHARLOTTE FEATHER

University of Sunderland, UK

Keywords: Queer leadership in academia; early-career academic challenges; LGBTQ+ inclusion in higher education; institutional power and marginalisation; queer pedagogy and mentorship; mental health and minority stress in academia

INTRODUCTION

Leadership in higher education (HE) is routinely framed within traditional paradigms of authority, experience and institutional allegiance. Yet, for queer academics, leadership does not necessarily arrive through formal promotion or official recognition. Instead, it often emerges though moments of advocacy, resistance and the everyday negotiations of power and identity within academic spaces. While early-career leadership can be a privilege – offering a platform for influence, visibility and professional growth – it can also expose individuals to heightened scrutiny, emotional labour and institutional resistance to those who challenge the status quo (Davies & Neustifter, 2023). Leadership in HE is rarely about stepping confidently into a role designed for you. More often, it is about navigating structures not built with you in mind and carving out legitimacy in spaces that still privilege cis-heteronormative ideas of leadership.

UK universities often position themselves as champions of inclusivity, but in the context of an increasingly neoliberal, marketised sector, LGBTQ+ inclusion is often top-down, tokenistic and performative – resulting in institutions that remain shaped by exclusionary norms (Barnett et al., 2013; Seal, 2019). Diversity is often welcomed only in its most palatable forms: when it does not disrupt too much, ask for too much or challenge too much. The paradox is that queer academics are often expected to be visible enough to 'represent' diversity initiatives but not so visible that they challenge dominant leadership frameworks (Sedgwick, 1990).

Leadership for LGBTQ+ academics becomes an ongoing process of resistance and redefinition where queer educators must perform a delicate balancing act of navigating expectations of authenticity, professionalism and institutional belonging (Gray, 2013; Pryor, 2020; Reinert & Yakaboski, 2017). This chapter explores these tensions, questioning what it means to lead as a queer early-career academic in an environment that demands diversity and, at times, resists it.

Theoretical Framing

Todorov's (1971) narrative theory of equilibrium suggests that narratives unfold through a cycle of stability, disruption, response and resolution. Though designed for literary analysis, it provides a useful metaphor for understanding queer early-career academics' navigation of leadership as they encounter moments of resistance, transformation and redefinition.

For queer early-career academics, the initial equilibrium reflects the early stages of academic life – securing a postdoctoral role, beginning a lectureship and building a research profile. During this phase, professional stability is often fragile, masked by unspoken tensions around perceived credibility and personal visibility (McCune, 2021). Following Todorov's cycle, disruptions emerge when queerness collides with institutional expectations, demanding adaptation without sacrificing authenticity. The challenge is not simply finding a resolution but developing sustainable pathways for impactful queer leadership.

Consider a queer early-career academic stepping into leadership. They may have been encouraged to lead a DEI committee or spearhead inclusivity initiatives, roles that appear affirming, but often reinforce institutional expectations of who 'does' diversity work (Ahmed, 2012). Meanwhile, they are navigating the subtle power dynamics of departmental meetings where their voice is heard but not always heeded; the academic finds themselves simultaneously visible and invisible. This chapter explores these disruptions in queer leadership, foregrounding personal responses and institutional resolutions that reshape, rather than merely restore, equilibrium.

THE DISRUPTIONS

Leading From the Margins

Leadership for queer early-career academics is shaped as much by power and belonging as by formal promotion.

Traditional HE leadership trajectories are presented as linear, marked by official promotions and institutional recognition. These models privilege visibility, assertiveness and adherence to dominant norms. However, for queer academics, leadership may manifest in more complex ways. Many will engage with informal leadership – through mentoring, DEI work and advocacy – long before they step into an officially recognised leadership role. These roles are vital to institutional culture but are not always recognised as 'real' leadership, positioning queer leaders as symbolic figures for inclusion while limiting access to formal advancement.

This dynamic is especially concerning in a sector marked by precarity, short-term contracts and performance metrics. Structural pressures disproportionately affect minoritised and early-career academics, intensifying experiences of exclusion and limiting progression (Bonello & Wånggren, 2023; O'Keefe & Courtois, 2019; UCU, 2021). Unlike traditional leadership models that reward conformity, queer leadership often arises from disruption (Gumbs, 2016; Pryor, 2020). It resists binaries, questions hierarchies and foregrounds relationships, care and ethics. Queering leadership is not about naming queer leaders, but about reimagining leadership itself. It emphasises collaboration over hierarchy, advocacy over neutrality and growth over preservation (Fagan, 2023; Ford et al., 2008; Harding et al., 2011). The question, then, is not only how queer academics navigate existing structures but also how they challenge who is allowed to lead and what leadership should look like.

Hyphenated Identities

The hyphen that sits between 'early' and 'career' is a metaphor for in-betweenness, a liminal space between being a newcomer and a leader. It signals contradiction: confidence and doubt, autonomy and dependency, innovation and conformity. Early-career leaders exist in a state of becoming, shaped by hierarchy and institutional culture while trying to assert credibility. This position can be both precarious and transformative. However, for queer early-career academics, the hyphen is also a site of resistance. Queerness entails a refusal of fixed categories and a constant negotiation of norms. To be queer and early-career is to experience compounded marginality – it seems you are often too new to lead, too different to belong.

Living in this space can be isolating and, for some, they must weigh the risks and consequences of being out, or being read, in leadership spaces constrained by politics of respectability and institutional cultures of sameness (McCune, 2021). Yet this position also offers a unique vantage point. Drawing from lived experience, queer leaders can question dominant paradigms, foster inclusivity and lead with a heightened awareness of belonging. Leadership in this space is relational and reflective, being redefined not as a pause before power, but as an ongoing reimagining of it. In this way, the queer early-career leader embodies a unique kind of hyphenated identity – one that resists closure, embraces multiplicity and redefines what it means to lead from the margins.

Institutional Power Dynamics

Power in HE is deeply embedded in structures that determine who is seen as a legitimate leader, who has access to career progression and whose expertise is valued. For queer early-career academics, these structures often manifest as gatekeeping, where leadership opportunities and promotions are shaped by implicit biases (Eliason, 2023). This is further compounded by the intersections of gender and race, with women and people of colour systematically underrepresented in senior academic and leadership positions (Arday et al., 2022; Arday & Mirza, 2018; Shepherd, 2017). Gatekeeping is not always overt and can exist in the informal networks where leadership potential is assessed, in the unspoken criteria that favour those who align with traditional academic norms and in the way certain research fields are dismissed as 'niche' or 'activist' rather than scholarly. Queer academics who engage in work related to gender, sexuality or social justice may find their contributions undervalued in funding applications reinforcing the notion that leadership is reserved for those who remain apolitical.

Beyond career progression, queer academics also navigate micro-level power dynamics in their everyday interactions. They may find that their authority is questioned in meetings or that they are expected to 'prove' their leadership capabilities in ways that their cis-heterosexual colleagues are not. Institutional power must be navigated with caution. Some queer academics seek to work within the system, aligning with traditional leadership expectations to gain influence. Others take a more radical approach, disrupting established norms and advocating for alternative leadership models.

MENTAL HEALTH AND BURNOUT

Two significant and interrelated disruptions that queer early-career leaders may face are mental ill-health and burnout. LGBTQ+ people are more likely to experience mental health challenges than their cisgender, heterosexual counterparts (Bai et al., 2024; Jaspal et al., 2023; Stonewall, 2018). This disparity is not inherent to queerness, but is often a consequence of systemic marginalisation, stigma and identity-based stressors that go unnoticed in professional environments.

For queer early-career academics, workplace pressures may be intensified by the emotional labour of managing marginalisation, negotiating visibility and responding to unspoken demands of informal leadership. Leadership, in this context, is not only about decision-making or influence. It is about endurance, emotional regulation and reflexivity. It is not just the workload that wears down capacity, but the emotional complexity of sustaining that work within systems that feel indifferent, or even hostile, to their presence.

Queer leaders in HE may find themselves under pressure to conform to dominant norms, mask aspects of their identity or temper their views to avoid being perceived as 'too disruptive' or 'too political'. This dissonance between authenticity and performativity can result in a form of identity-related strain known as minority stress (Meyer, 2003; Meyer & Frost, 2013). Unlike general workplace stress, minority stress stems from systemic inequalities, yet it is rarely acknowledged in leadership discourses, which tend to privilege productivity over well-being, and performance over personhood.

What is often overlooked in institutional narratives about leadership resilience is the invisible toll of constantly managing how one is seen, heard and judged. For some, the cost of showing up authentically becomes too high. For others, invisibility breeds isolation and erodes mental health over time. Moreover, concerns about being viewed as less competent, less stable or 'not ready' for leadership can deter queer academics from seeking help when they need it most. In this way, the silence surrounding mental health becomes a mechanism of discipline, forcing individuals to internalise structural harms as personal failings. And yet, it is precisely here that queer early-career leaders are uniquely positioned to foster emotionally literate and compassionate leadership cultures. Experiences of navigating marginalisation and precarity cultivates a heightened sensitivity to exclusion, burnout and belonging. This emotional attunement, rooted not in formal training but in lived resilience (Meyer, 2015), can form the basis of a deeply compassionate leadership practice that places care and connection at its core (Snyder, 2006). By leading with empathy, queer academics can challenge the detachment of academic professionalism and reframe leadership as an inter-personal and restorative act.

PERSONAL RESPONSES

The earlier sections of this chapter have explored the disruptions that shape early-career leadership: the marginalisation of informal leadership; the experience of hyphenated identity; institutional gatekeeping; the emotional and mental toll of visibility and the unrecognised weight of advocacy. While these accounts underscore the weight of the challenges queer early-career leaders may encounter, they also lay the groundwork for what comes next: an exploration of the resourceful, resilient and imaginative responses that arise in the face of adversity. In this section, the focus shifts to those responses – the creative, critical and strategic practices through which queer leaders navigate, negotiate and reshape their leadership trajectories. These responses do not restore a presumed or prior equilibrium, nor do they erase the structural conditions that continue to constrain. Instead, they forge a new, queered equilibrium: one that centres authenticity, community and resistance.

Whilst Lee's (2020) work focused on school leaders, her argument that LGBTQ+ educators possess a particular repertoire of skills conducive to excellent leadership, resonates in HE. Queer early-career leaders often bring heightened emotional intelligence, cultural sensitivity, adaptability and an unwavering commitment to equity. These are not supplementary attributes, but core capacities that enable ethical and impactful leadership, even, and perhaps especially, in the absence of formal authority.

Visibility and Risk: Navigating When and How to Be Seen

One common response to disruption is a strategic relationship with visibility. For many queer early-career leaders, visibility can be both empowering and risky. Leadership responses often involve carefully choosing when, where and how to be visible – particularly in institutions that celebrate diversity rhetorically but remain slow to transform structurally.

> *Vignette 1: Layla*
> Layla, a lesbian academic, chose to be visibly 'out' in her teaching and public-facing work, embedding queer theory into her curriculum and listing her pronouns and advocacy work in her bio. However, when invited to speak on an DEI panel during Pride Month, she declined, focusing her time instead on an LGBTQ+ mentorship initiative that contributed to structural change.

Layla's narrative reflects a common tension. Queer leaders often feel a deep responsibility to represent and support others but are also acutely aware when visibility risks becoming symbolic rather than systemic. One of the ways to respond to this disruption is to set boundaries, redistribute your energy and choose how and where your leadership is most impactful. This intentional negotiation of visibility is not a retreat from power; it is a redefinition of it. Queer early-career leaders are not less capable of leadership. Rather, they are often more aware of its complexities. They understand that leadership is not only about being *seen* but also about being *effective*. It is knowing when to speak, when to listen and when to channel influence through quieter forms of institutional change. In this way, queer leadership makes space for visibility that is grounded in integrity and invisibility that is chosen, not imposed. This leadership style marks the emergence of a new, queered equilibrium, one where leadership is not determined by optics, but by ethics and critical agency.

Everyday Influence: Claiming Leadership in the Informal

When traditional leadership roles are inaccessible, many queer early-career academics claim leadership outside formal structures through mentoring, advocacy and inclusive pedagogical change. These roles, while often unrecognised in metrics, are integral to institutional culture. Rather than aspiring to hierarchy, queer leaders often cultivate horizontal influence, leading through connection, care and mutual support. This reframes leadership not as position but as *practice*.

> ***Vignette 2: Marcus***
> Marcus, a Black gay doctoral researcher, became a central figure for students and junior colleagues through consistent acts of mentorship and advocacy such as co-facilitating peer writing groups and organising events for LGBTQ+ students of colour. Though his work went unrecognised in evaluations, his impact on students' sense of belonging was undeniable. Marcus exercised leadership by building trust and cultivating spaces where others could thrive. For him, leadership was not about recognition but about doing the work that mattered in the everyday.

Marcus' story illustrates how queer early-career leadership often operates outside formal recognition yet holds transformative potential. Drawing on queer theory's resistance to rigid structures and linear progression, Marcus' actions exemplify a leadership practice that is emergent and collective. It is precisely this informal influence, unmeasured but deeply felt, that redefines what it means to lead from the margins (Rottmann, 2006).

Collective Care: Building Queer Networks of Support

Another response to institutional disruption is the creation of peer-based, community-driven networks. Recognising the limitations of traditional mentorship structures, queer early-career leaders are increasingly turning to alternative models of support and knowledge-exchange. Networks can offer both emotional sustenance and practical support, enabling queer academics to navigate their institutions with solidarity rather than in isolation. These informal collectives often operate as spaces of refuge and resource, embodying a queer ethic of leadership that values interdependence over competition. As Freeman (2010) argues, queer time operates outside of linear progress – it values process over product, care over control and becoming over achievement. Through these networks, queer leaders construct new equilibria not by assimilating, but by reimagining what leadership looks like from the ground up.

> *Vignette 3: Clodagh*
> Clodagh, a queer, neurodivergent academic, found the formal structures of their institution isolating. They rarely saw themselves reflected in leadership and struggled to access mentorship. In response, Clodagh created an online collective for LGBTQ+ early-career academics. The group operated informally and without a hierarchy, allowing Clodagh to find the solidarity they had been seeking.

Clodagh's story highlights the power of networks grounded in mutual support and reciprocity. Rather than replicating institutional models of mentorship or leadership, these collectives prioritise relationality, shared vulnerability and the redistribution of knowledge and power. In doing so, they embody a distinctly queer ethic of leadership in environments that champion individualism.

Pedagogical Disruption: Teaching as Leadership Practice

Many queer early-career academics assert leadership through inclusive, transformative pedagogies. The HE classroom becomes a site of radical possibility where queer ways of knowing are legitimised and analysed. Through curriculum design and critical reflexivity, queer leaders shape cultures of belonging that ripple outward, impacting student experiences and broader academic environments.

> ***Vignette 4: Yusef***
> Yusef, a bisexual early-career academic, approached his classroom as a space for transformation. He redesigned the curriculum to foreground queer and decolonial voices, utilising literature that had been previously absent from the reading list. Rather than positioning himself as the sole authority, Yusef encouraged students to co-create learning materials and influence the seminar content. Students named his classroom as uniquely inclusive and intellectually challenging. This catalysed a shift in departmental practices as colleagues began adopting his methods. Though Yusef held no formal leadership role, his pedagogy fostered belonging, agency and critical questioning.

Yusef's approach illustrates how pedagogical leadership serves as a powerful, if understated, form of queer disruption. Rooted in co-production and reflexivity, his teaching aligns with hooks' (1994) concept of *engaged pedagogy* – a practice that centres intellectual and emotional presence. This leadership reconfigures the classroom as a site of collective transformation and unsettling norms, cultivating spaces where knowledge is relational and identity is not bracketed out (Rottmann, 2006). Through values-driven pedagogy, queer early-career academics like Yusef catalyse ripple effects that shift departmental cultures from within.

From Response to Queered Equilibrium

In Todorov's model, equilibrium is not a return to the original state but a transformation – a new balance shaped by disruption. For queer early-career leaders, the strategies outlined above do not eliminate structural barriers, but they do establish a *queered equilibrium*: one grounded in resilience, relationality and resistance. This equilibrium is a process of continual negotiation. It requires adapting and reimagining leadership in ways that remain authentic under pressure. Thus, queer leadership is not a fixed status but an ongoing practice.

INSTITUTIONAL RESOLUTIONS

While queer early-career academics model resilience, adaptability and ethical leadership, the burden of structural change must not rest with them alone. Institutions must move beyond what Ahmed (2004, p. 3) terms 'non-performatives' – policies that declare commitment to diversity without enacting meaningful change – and take seriously their role in dismantling the barriers that constrain queer leadership in HE (Veldhuis, 2020). Universities need to expand their understanding of leadership to recognise informal and equity-driven practices. This work must be embedded in workload models, recognised in promotion criteria and integrated into leadership development, not treated as optional or symbolic.

Furthermore, targeted leadership programmes for LGBTQ+ and other marginalised staff are essential. These should centre intersectionality, provide mentoring and sponsorship and offer identity-affirming spaces for growth. Leadership potential must be recognised not by conformity to dominant norms, but by the capacity to lead with integrity, reflexivity and cultural competence. Institutions must also centre wellbeing as a core leadership value. This requires challenging competitive, performative cultures and addressing the structural conditions that produce burnout and minority stress. A culture of care backed by policy, resources and accountability is fundamental.

Finally, institutions must be willing to be queered – to embrace disruption, challenge normative assumptions and reimagine leadership not as hierarchy but as shared, adaptive and ethically grounded.

CONCLUSION

Queer early-career academics in HE occupy a complex and generative space. As this chapter has shown, queer leadership often emerges not through formal recognition but through disruption: of norms, of structures and of what leadership is imagined to be. Navigating the hyphen between early and career, these individuals lead in ways that are relational, reflective and radically situated. Through strategic visibility, informal influence, boundary-setting, collective organising and inclusive pedagogy, queer early-career leaders are not simply surviving institutions, they are quietly and powerfully transforming them. Their leadership challenges dominant paradigms by centring community and revealing the potential for a more expansive, more ethical model of academic leadership. And yet, this labour cannot be carried alone. There is a need for institutions to recognise that these acts of leadership are essential to more just and inclusive educational spaces. The responsibility for change must shift from the individuals who embody difference to the systems that have historically excluded it. To que(e)ry leadership, then, is to refuse narrow definitions of success, to disrupt binary thinking and to embrace leadership as an evolving, shared practice. Queer early-career academics are already enacting this vision of leadership; the task now is for institutions to catch up.

REFERENCES

Ahmed, S. (2004). Declarations of whiteness: The non-performativity of anti-racism. *Borderlands*, *3*(2).

Ahmed, S. (2012). *On being included: Racism and diversity in institutional life*. Duke University Press.

Arday, J., Branchu, C., & Boliver, V. (2022). What do we know about black and minority ethnic (BME) participation in UK higher education. *Social Policy and Society*, *21* (1), 12–25.

Arday, J., & Mirza, H. (Eds.). (2018). *Dismantling race in higher education: Racism, whiteness and decolonising the academy*. Palgrave Macmillan.

Bai, Y., Kim, C., Levitskaya, E., Burneiko, N., Lenciu, K., & Chum, A. (2024). Long-term trends in mental health disparities across sexual orientations in the UK: A longitudinal analysis (2010–2021). *Social Psychiatry and Psychiatric Epidemiology*. https://doi.org/10.1007/s00127-024-02751-w

Barnett, R., Parry, G., & Coate, K. (2013). *Conceptualising curriculum change: New directions for the learning society*. Open University Press.

Bonello, M., & Wånggren, L. (2023). *Working conditions in a marketised university system: Generation precarity*. Palgrave Macmillan.

Davies, A. W., & Neustifter, R. (2023). Heteroprofessionalism in the academy: The surveillance and regulation of queer faculty in higher education. *Journal of Homosexuality*, 70(6), 1030–1054.

Eliason, M. J. (2023). Queer faculty in the academy: Is it getting better? *Journal of Homosexuality*, 71(11), 2507–2532.

Fagan, J. C. (2023). Transgender and gender non-conforming leaders and leadership: A foundational and integrative review. *JMU Libraries*, 243(1), 1–45.

Ford, J., Harding, N., & Learmonth, M. (2008). Queer(y)ing leadership. In *Leadership as identity* (pp. 91–115). Palgrave Macmillan. https://doi.org/10.1057/9780230584181_5

Freeman, E. (2010). *Time binds: Queer temporalities, queer histories*. Duke University Press.

Gray, E. M. (2013). Coming out as a lesbian, gay or bisexual teacher: Negotiating private and professional worlds. *Sex Education*, 13(6), 702–714.

Gumbs, A. P. (2016). Introduction. In A. P. Gumbs, C. Martens, & M. Williams (Eds.), *Revolutionary mothering: Love on the front lines*. PM Press.

Harding, N., Hugh, L., Ford, J., & Learnmouth, M. (2011). Leadership and charisma: A desire that cannot speak its name? *Human Relations, 64*(7), 927–949.

hooks, b. (1994). *Teaching to transgress: Education as the practice of freedom*. Routledge.

Jaspal, R., Lopes, B., & Breakwell, G. M. (2023). Minority stressors, protective factors and mental health outcomes in lesbian, gay and bisexual people in the UK. *Current Psychology, 42*, 24918–24934.

Lee, C. (2020, July). Why LGBT teachers make exceptional school leaders. *Frontiers in Education*. https://doi.org/10.3389/fsoc.2020.00050

McCune, V. (2021). Academic identities in contemporary higher education: Sustaining identities that value teaching. *Teaching in Higher Education, 26*(1), 20–35.

Meyer, I. H. (2003). Prejudice, social stress, and mental health in lesbian, gay, and bisexual populations: Conceptual issues and research evidence. *Psychological Bulletin, 129*, 674–697.

Meyer, I. H. (2015). Resilience in the study of minority stress and health of sexual and gender minorities. *Psychology of Sexual Orientation and Gender Diversity, 2*, 209.

Meyer, I. H., & Frost, D. M. (2013). Minority stress and the health of sexual minorities. In C. J. Patterson & A. R. D'Augelli (Eds.), *Handbook of psychology and sexual orientation* (pp. 252–266). Oxford University Press.

O'Keefe, T., & Courtois, A. (2019). 'Not one of the family': Gender and precarious work in the neoliberal university. *Gender, Work and Organization*, 26(4), 463–479.

Pryor, J. T. (2020). Queer advocacy leadership: A queer leadership model for higher education. *Journal of Leadership Education*, 19(1), 69–81.

Reinert, L., & Yakaboski, T. (2017). Being out matters for lesbian faculty: Personal identities influence professional experiences. *NASPA Journal About Women in Higher Education*, 10(3), 319–336.

Rottmann, C. (2006). Queering educational leadership from the inside out. *International Journal of Leadership in Education*, 9(1), 1–20.

Seal, M. (2019). *The interruption of heteronormativity in higher education, queer and critical pedagogies*. Queer studies and education. Palgrave Macmillan.

Sedgwick, E. K. (1990). *Epistemology of the closet*. University of California Press.

Shepherd, S. (2017). Why are there so few female leaders in higher education: A case of structure or agency? *Management in Education*, 31(2), 82–87.

Snyder, K. (2006). *The G Quotient: Why gay executives are excelling as leaders and what every manager needs to know*. Jossey-Bass.

Stonewall. (2018). *LGBT in Britain – University report*. https://www.stonewall.org.uk/resources/lgbt-britain-university-report-2018

Todorov, T. (1971). The 2 principles of narrative. *Diacritics*, 1(1), 37–44.

University and College Union (UCU). (2021). *Challenging LGBT+ exclusion in UK higher education*. https://doi.org/ https://www.ucu.org.uk/media/11495/Challenging-LGBT-exclusion-in-UK-higher-education/pdf/LGBT__exclusion_May2021.pdf

Veldhuis, C. (2020). Doubly marginalized: Addressing the minority stressors experienced by LGBTQ+ researchers who do LGBTQ+ research. *Health Education & Behavior*, 49(6), 960–974.

12

EMPOWERING LGBTQ+ LEADERS IN HIGHER EDUCATION: NAVIGATING IDENTITY, INCLUSION AND CAREER PROGRESSION

CATHERINE LEE AND DANIEL BURMAN

Anglia Ruskin University, UK

Keywords: LGBTQ+ leadership development programme in UK higher education; LGBTQ+ leadership development programme findings; motivation for participating in LGBTQ+ leadership development programme; inspiring, nurturing and developing LGBTQ+ leadership; LGBTQ+ network building

INTRODUCTION

Effective university leadership hinges on a deep understanding of human behaviour, the ability to clearly communicate goals and the capacity to inspire individuals to adopt behaviours that facilitate goal achievement (Ruben et al., 2023; Sashkin & Sashkin, 2003). In the United Kingdom, universities are often steeped in tradition, particularly among prestigious Russell Group universities, where research has historically taken precedence over teaching and is fundamental to career progression (Goodall, 2009).

The landscape of higher education in the United Kingdom has evolved significantly since 1992, following the reclassification of polytechnics as universities and the introduction of league tables to monitor institutional performance. Increasing emphasis has been placed on student outcomes, including attainment, satisfaction, employability and access. Teaching quality is now formally assessed through the Teaching Excellence Framework (TEF), mirroring the long-standing evaluation of research through the Research Excellence Framework (REF).

As the financial model for universities transitioned from government grants to student fees, prospective students have become more discerning in their university choices. Consequently, a 'buyer's market' has emerged outside the most prestigious universities, influencing the leadership competencies required within higher education.

Despite the increasing complexity of university leadership, resistance remains regarding the appointment of individuals from non-academic backgrounds (Spendlove, 2007). Goodall (2009) found that the highest-ranked universities are frequently led by individuals with extensive research citations. Similarly, Yielder and Codling (2004) note that within traditional universities, academic distinction remains the primary criterion for leadership progression, often taking precedence over managerial competence.

However, some institutions have begun to recognise and nurture leadership potential from a more diverse talent pool.

In 2021, Lee noted that a handful of Higher Education Institutions had taken early steps towards identifying and developing leadership skills among employees from varied backgrounds. Data from *Times Higher Education* (2023) revealed that among the world's top 200 universities, 48 vice-chancellors were women, a 12% increase from the previous year and a 41% rise over five years. Despite this progress, only three vice-chancellors were from Black, Asian or minority ethnic backgrounds, and no formal data currently exist on vice-chancellors from LGBTQ+ communities.

According to the 2023 *Advance HE Equality in Higher Education* report, 47% of university staff identified as heterosexual, while smaller percentages identified as bisexual (1.6%), gay male (1.4%), lesbian or gay female (0.7%) or transgender (0.5%). The percentages in these data clearly show that much of the HE workforce is not represented at all, suggesting many prefer not to record their sexuality of gender identity in their university workplace.

While Advance HE has implemented leadership programmes to support women and people of colour, no national tailored programme currently exists for aspiring LGBTQ+ university leaders. In the academic year 2022–2023, one post-92 university introduced a leadership development initiative specifically designed for LGBTQ+ staff seeking progression into middle and senior management roles, and this chapter reports the findings from the programme.

The chapter begins with a description of the leadership programme and participant profiles. The methodological approach is then presented before the findings are revealed and discussed. Concluding remarks bring the chapter to a close and offer recommendations for further research into leadership development strategies.

THE LGBTQ+ LEADERSHIP DEVELOPMENT PROGRAMME

The LGBTQ+ university leadership development programme was informed by a prior initiative supporting LGBTQ+ leadership in schools (Lee, 2020). Designed with input from two focus groups of LGBTQ+ university staff, the programme was structured around five key areas:

- Inspirational LGBTQ+ leadership narratives.
- Developing leadership identity and practice.
- Communication and presentation skills.
- Overcoming barriers and driving institutional change.
- Networking and community building.

The programme aimed to address the challenges faced by LGBTQ+ academics and professionals in universities while leveraging the strengths they have developed through navigating these challenges. Over an academic year, 12 participants engaged in three in-person leadership development sessions. Participants worked one-on-one with one of 7 mentors, each an LGBTQ+ leader with extensive experience in higher education to refine their leadership goals.

Participants were recruited through Human Resources channels and the university's LGBTQ+ staff network. Open to both academic and professional services staff, the programme required participants to obtain managerial approval, indicating that they were already out to some extent within the workplace. The programme excluded senior executives within the university's leadership team.

METHODOLOGY

This research is grounded in a phenomenological framework (Husserl, 1999), which seeks to uncover the structures and meanings embedded in lived experiences. Phenomenology was chosen as it allows for an in-depth exploration of participants' subjective perspectives. Traditionally, phenomenological research employs open-ended interviews; however, in this study, participants provided written reflections via anonymous evaluation forms completed after each leadership development session. Allowing for anonymous evaluation enhanced psychological safety for participants and fostered open communication and actionable feedback.

The evaluation process served three primary functions. First, it allowed facilitators to assess participant experiences in real time, ensuring that the programme evolved to meet their needs. Second, it encouraged participants to reflect critically on their progress, fostering continuous engagement between sessions. Finally, it generated qualitative data tracking the participants' leadership development over the course of the programme.

The authors had dual roles as programme facilitators and researchers. As members of the LGBTQ+ community, we bring personal lived experiences that shape our interpretation of the data, and our direct engagement adds contextual richness to the analysis.

The dataset consisted of three evaluation responses from each of the 12 participants. Data analysis followed Carspecken's (2001) emergent coding methodology. Initial thematic coding identified four key areas: confidence-building, networking, leveraging the experience of being marginalised and setting and pursuing leadership goals. Further analysis using Carspecken's critical approach led to the identification of additional themes, including the impact of mentorship, behavioural changes resulting from the programme and the application of newly developed leadership skills.

This methodological approach allowed for an in-depth exploration of how participants engaged with the programme and how it influenced their professional trajectories.

RESULTS

Table 12.1 presents a profile of each of the 12 participants, including their identity, tenure at the university, role, career goal and details of the promotion they sought and whether this was achieved.

Motivation for Participating in the Programme

The primary reason for applying for the programme was the aspiration for career progression and leadership opportunities. One lesbian participant expressed that while she did not yet feel prepared for a leadership role, she viewed the programme as a foundational step in developing the readiness required when an appropriate opportunity arose. Several participants sought to cultivate leadership qualities, with one gay man in professional services aiming to 'gain insight into the leadership qualities needed'. Across the spectrum of lesbian, non-binary and gay male participants, there was a shared interest in developing skills to be effective managers and increasing their confidence in embodying leadership.

Another key motivation was access to mentorship. A gay male lecturer hoped that his mentor would assist in 'identifying goals, developing strategies, and setting a pathway to leadership'. Three participants in professional services roles

Table 12.1. Profile of the Participants

Self-Declared Identity	Time at the University	Role at the Start of the Programme	Career Goal at Outset of Programme	Applied for Promotion	Promotion Achieved During the Programme
Lesbian	13 years	Academic partnership manager	Academic partnership director	Yes	Additional DEI leadership
Transgender	7 months	SU campaigns coordinator	SU leadership	No	No
Gay man	3 years	Course leader drama	Deputy head of school	No	No
Gay man	6 months	Lecturer in biomedical sciences	Senior lecturer	Yes	Senior lecturer
Gay man	3 years	Lecturer in biomedical science	Senior lecturer	Yes	No
Non-binary	3 years	Lecturer in digital media	Course leader	Yes	Course leader
Gay man	3 years	Senior research fellow	Associate professor	Yes	No
Gay man	6 months	Technical analyst	Senior technical analyst	Yes	Senior technical analyst and study

(Continued)

Table 12.1. (Continued)

Self-Declared Identity	Time at the University	Role at the Start of the Programme	Career Goal at Outset of Programme	Applied for Promotion	Promotion Achieved During the Programme
Lesbian	7 years	Lecturer in business	Senior lecturer	Yes	Senior lecturer
Gay man	1 year	Online technician	Technician team leader	No	No
Lesbian	18 months	Executive assistant	Project leader	No	Began part-time masters study
Gay man	7 years	Business manager	Senior business manager	Yes	Senior business manager

Source: Lee and Burman (2024).

sought advice on navigating leadership while being openly LGBTQ+ in the workplace, while a lesbian professional services staff member sought guidance in compiling a compelling CV. The non-binary participant wished to learn how to succeed in leadership while feeling like an 'outsider,' acknowledging a perceived lack of institutional belonging.

A strong theme in the participants' motivations was the desire for networking opportunities within the university LGBTQ+ community. More than half of the cohort expressed a need for kinship, shared experiences and a sense of belonging. Some shared that before the programme, they knew few, if any, other LGBTQ+ colleagues within the institution.

When asked about their learning objectives for the programme, many aimed to deepen their understanding of leadership within the unique culture of higher education. One gay male lecturer wanted to build confidence and receive support as he pursued a promotion. A lesbian professional services participant sought assistance with interview skills and presentation techniques, while another wanted to understand leadership theory and plan their career trajectory. The non-binary participant sought to refine their communication and presentation techniques, while a lesbian lecturer wished for greater confidence in decision-making. Two of the gay men were interested in identifying their strengths and weaknesses and learning how to harness their abilities as future leaders.

Out of 12 participants, 8 applied for promotion during the programme, with 6 successfully securing advancement. Two others embarked on part-time postgraduate study to enhance their career prospects. While the programme was not exclusively designed for career advancement, it aimed to build self-confidence, promote authenticity in the workplace and provide opportunities to practice leadership behaviours.

Among those who were not promoted, one lesbian professional services participant enrolled in an MSc in Psychology, and another began actively seeking new roles, stating she was now 'pursuing opportunities I previously wouldn't have considered'.

Emerging Themes From Programme Feedback

As the programme progressed, participant feedback revealed four primary areas in which they felt supported:

- Confidence in their leadership abilities.
- Networking and building community.
- Harnessing the power of being different.
- Pursuing leadership goals.

Each of these themes is explored below, drawing from participant evaluations.

Confidence in Leadership Abilities

Confidence-building emerged as a dominant theme in participant feedback. The programme facilitated self-reflection, enabling participants to identify their strengths and areas for growth as emerging leaders. Two gay male participants described how they confronted their 'imposter syndrome' and developed self-assurance in their professional environments. Changes in workplace behaviours included being more decisive, communicating more directly, setting clearer boundaries, demonstrating resilience and embracing vulnerability. One lesbian academic renegotiated her professional objectives with her line manager, explaining:

> *I have had a complete restructure of responsibilities with appraisal objectives focused on moving up within the university.*

This shift indicated renewed ambition and alignment between her personal and professional identities (Lee, 2021), enabling career progression with confidence. A lesbian professional services participant reflected:

> *Through this programme, I have learned to reflect on my own qualities, derived from lived experiences, and I'm beginning to see them as strengths.*

A key message of the programme was that LGBTQ+ lived experiences often cultivate attributes valuable for transformational leadership. Research by Lee (2020) on LGBTQ+ aspiring school leaders found that navigating heteronormative and cisnormative work environments can develop emotional intelligence, inclusion awareness, team-building skills, adaptability and courage, qualities crucial for leadership.

Networking and Building Community

The year-long leadership programme provided a unique networking space for LGBTQ+ professionals within the university. Participants valued the chance to connect with LGBTQ+ colleagues and learn from experienced LGBTQ+ leaders. One non-binary academic described the programme as a 'fantastic opportunity to meet more LGBTQ+ professionals'. There was a notable distinction between this programme and the university's existing LGBTQ+ staff network. Some participants perceived the staff network as inherently political, feeling hesitant to join out of concern that membership might necessitate being openly out to the entire university community. However, through the programme, some participants reframed their views and ultimately joined the staff network during the programme. A gay male academic commented:

> *This leadership programme made me rethink the importance of my visibility as a role model. Visibility doesn't always have to be political.*

Harnessing the Power of Being Different

Participants were encouraged to view their LGBTQ+ identity as an asset in leadership. The programme highlighted that navigating professional spaces as an LGBTQ+ person fosters skills such as emotional intelligence, inclusion awareness and adaptability. A gay male academic noted:

> *The programme enabled me to leverage my LGBTQ+ identity to become a more effective leader.*

A professional services participant shared:

> *Taking part in the programme helped me realise that my queer identity is a strength, not a limitation.*

Pursuing Leadership Goals

Using Whitmore's (2010) GROW model, participants mapped out leadership goals with their mentors. A lesbian professional services participant who secured a new DEI role wrote:

> *My mentor was incredible. We discussed job applications, interviews, authenticity, and navigating professional boundaries.*

Participants overwhelmingly found the programme valuable. By the final session, the group referred to it as their 'safe space'. A gay male academic stated:

The programme allowed me to explore vulnerability and build strengths to pursue leadership roles.

This study suggests that targeted leadership programmes for LGBTQ+ employees are crucial in higher education. They provide safe environments for self-exploration, mentorship and career development, allowing participants to embrace leadership as their authentic selves.

CONCLUDING REMARKS

This study has illustrated the significant role that LGBTQ+-focused leadership development can play in higher education, providing an affirming and inclusive environment where university staff can reflect on their leadership aspirations and professional growth. Its impact extended far beyond career advancement. In the final evaluation, all participants expressed appreciation for the safe space created by the initiative. Several participants conveyed an unexpected sense of relief at not having to navigate the complexities of coming out in a new setting, with two stating that the programme's inherent inclusivity allowed them to focus entirely on their development. Several participants also described the programme as a space where they formed lifelong friendships and a strong sense of professional community.

This leadership programme represented a tangible investment by the university in its LGBTQ+ employees, demonstrating a commitment to their professional development and career progression. The existence of such a programme signalled the institution's support for LGBTQ+ staff aspiring to leadership roles.

As this study is based on a single university, broader generalisations should be approached with caution. However, there remains a need for further research into the impact and effectiveness of LGBTQ+-specific leadership development initiatives. The 2023 *Advance HE Equality in Higher Education* report indicated that nearly half of university staff chose not to disclose their sexual orientation or gender identity to their employer. The reasons for this remain complex and difficult to quantify, but it is reasonable to suggest that universities must do more to foster environments where LGBTQ+ employees feel safe, valued and able to be their authentic selves.

REFERENCES

Carspecken, P. F. (2001). Critical ethnographies from Houston: Distinctive features and directions. In P. F. Carspecken & G. Walford (Eds.), *Critical ethnography and education* (pp. 1–26). Emerald Group Publishing Limited.

Goodall, A. H. (2009). Highly cited leaders and the performance of research universities. *Research Policy*, *38*(7), 1079–1092.

Husserl, E. (1999). *The essential Husserl: Basic writings in transcendental phenomenology*. Indiana University Press.

Lee, C. (2020). Courageous leaders: Promoting and supporting diversity in school leadership development. *Management in Education*, *34*(1), 5–15.

Lee, C. (2021). Promoting diversity in university leadership: The argument for LGBTQ+ specific leadership programmes in higher education. *Perspectives: Policy and Practice in Higher Education*, *25*(3), 91–99.

Lee, C., & Burman, D. (2024). 'I have gained insight, direction, affirmation, and a network'. Examining the impact of the UK's first LGBTQ+ specific leadership development programme in higher education. *Educational Management Administration & Leadership.* https://doi.org/10.1177/17411432241260946

Ruben, B. D., De Lisi, R., & Gigliotti, R. A. (2023). *A guide for leaders in higher education: Concepts, competencies, and tools.* Taylor & Francis.

Sashkin, M., & Sashkin, M. G. (2003). *Leadership that matters: The critical factors for making a difference in people's lives and organizations' success.* Berrett-Koehler Publishers.

Spendlove, M. (2007). Competencies for effective leadership in higher education. *International Journal of Educational Management, 21*(5), 407–417.

Whitmore, J. (2010). *Coaching for performance: Growing human potential and purpose: The principles and practice of coaching and leadership.* Hachette UK.

Yielder, J., & Codling, A. (2004). Management and leadership in the contemporary university. *Journal of Higher Education Policy and Management, 26*(3), 315–328.

13

TEACHING THE FUTURE LEADERS: LEARNING AND TRAINING TO BECOME A SUCCESSFUL LGBTQ+ LEADER WITHIN HIGHER EDUCATION

HELEN BUSHELL-THORNALLEY

Bishop Grosseteste University, UK

Keywords: LGBTQ+ leadership; higher education; initial teacher education; ITE ITT; inclusive pedagogy; physical education and dance

This chapter offers a personal and reflective account of what it means to lead as an LGBTQ+ academic within the disciplines of Teacher Education, Physical Education, Sport, and Dance (PESSD). Through an autobiographical lens, I explore how my leadership is shaped by lived experience, particularly under the lingering legacy of Section 28 and the enduring presence of heteronormativity within educational and sporting environments. Readers are invited to consider how identity, authenticity and inclusion intersect with leadership practice in higher education. I weave together personal narratives, critical theory and professional experience to illuminate the challenges and possibilities of being a visible and values-driven LGBTQ+ leader in complex institutional landscapes.

My life outside of work had been highly successful within the paradigm of sport, where my true authentic self as an LGBTQ+ individual bore no relevance to selection and progression through the ranks. Aspiration was not only to get it right as a leader for my learners but also to inspire them to influence the next generation they would go on to teach. It could then be considered that I would have been able to seamlessly transfer the learnt leadership and performance skills into these new chapters of my professional life, but the reality was that on many occasions this was challenging.

Reflective questions are considered through an autobiographical interpretative position because of my experiences as a LGBTQ+ leader. By doing so the narratives of how I learnt to be a successful leader was through the often interchangeable skill sets I adopted illustrating how the entwined different aspects of my life liberated me during difficult times within the variety of my roles.

My philosophy has always been framed and observed as an educationalist who weaved work and leadership in ways that were deliberate, and by doing so passed the baton on for others to shape and create cultures that represented and protected diversity, equality and inclusion. These career principles now spanned a 30-year journey, it felt at times the shadows of the past still existed as selection (promotion) and deselection (rejection) was less about the competences of me being a leader and more about how my authentic characteristics may have been the downfall within a prescribed selection process. If this was the reality for me, I am sure it would have been the same for others in leadership who had similar characteristics (Lee, 2023). In addition to these leadership barriers, I was working in the subject domain that was mainly considered gender binary because of the discipline's performance traditions, where fluidity within these realities was often resisted.

There is a perceived notion about who is acceptable to achieve in certain leadership roles in PESSD, and it was less likely to be anyone from outside the favoured male heteronormative selection pool, where power and status seemed to be naturally awarded (Foucault, 1980). The barriers were stacked against me to reach my full potential within leadership when placed against another reality that within the United Kingdom, homophobia is still found within many walks of life.

I accepted leadership roles confidently, but I also knew I had to be afforded autonomy to achieve successes. This misrepresentation of LGBTQ+ females in PESSD leadership was true on many occasions in HE settings, and unfortunately a continuation of what I had found in my professional roles within school education systems. I thought it would have been easier as an HE colleague, because these institutions are seen as places that challenge the status quo. The Equality Act of 2010 had made a level of impact but authors on leadership and LGBTQ+ communities recognise that the cultural silhouettes of how systems work are very slow to change and extremely difficult to infiltrate.

These well-known professional development prospects are referred to in several interdisciplinary leadership sources such as the critical lenses of feminist and queer theories, where academics have proved inequality and professional development opportunities may be founded on gender and sexual orientation rather than the personal qualities of potential leaders (Morley, 2013). Irrespective of these challenges, on many occasions I was given the opportunity to lead colleagues, mainly male, trainee Secondary school PE teachers, and sports specialists who all had their perceptions of who they should be led by and who they would take direction from.

It was here that the reality became obvious that I was now performing in a panoptic framework where my decision-making was scrutinised as much through my character as it was through my direction. The position I found myself in as a senior lecturer was that these tasks held very similar expectations of criteria to the positions I had experienced as an elite athlete.

I had been in many large communities with goal-orientated individuals who all contributed to collective and personal objectives. Communities of practice were generated from within setting, and I had to orchestrate this from the front. HEIs in the United Kingdom are known to have greater educational autonomy over how programmes are constructed therefore those that serve materials to the learners have the potential to impart a great deal more from their own character and moral values.

Throughout my leadership and educational career one of the most persuasive comments for me was cited over 20 years ago by Michael Fullan (2016). Fullan uses an analogy on how true leadership is created through the capacity to not only drive the bus forward with a clear collective vision, but the bus must be full. This analogy encouraged me to ensure that the individuals I would be working with were not passive passenger in the new environments that I hoped to create or even worse they were not even getting on that bus with me because of what I stood for. Therefore, I used robust strategies that I knew worked and I became extremely astute and resourceful in using theories from the domain of cohesive performance when forming new group behaviours and challenging conflict (Tuckman, 2010). I also coupled this with survival techniques so I could begin to challenge mimicking behaviours of current beliefs with ideas to shape the new cultural ways.

I aligned my lived experiences to the Darwinist theorisation of cultural survival (Darwin, 2000). I crafted my early leadership style within HE into something that was not dissimilar to that of my school and playing careers because I knew even as a leader in a potentially more accepting environment, I had to be prepared to be disappointed.

I needed to read the opposition, other colleagues and learners within these settings who might be less forgiving to an LGBTQ+ female individual in a position of power. Oppositional challenges were different from those that I had previously been confronted with as a schoolteacher; DfE, Ofsted, examination boards and the unique historical culture of the school. HEI systems do not exist in quite the same way, yes, they are internally and externally scrutinised, but large parts of content, delivery modes and assessments are driven, often within and through the reflection of those in the settings.

Differing ways of thinking are difficult to manage. However, I quickly learnt that the individuals I would be working with would play a crucial part in my successes and failures in these roles. Therefore, for my leadership to be effective, I needed to reach these goals through a shared vision, as I aimed to foster an inclusive culture that was embraced by the entire team.

I had achieved success with this strategy, and I did at various times become that different voice and encouraged others to do the same (Bushell-Thornalley, 2025). I was confident that if there was a synergy of programme creation and delivery, colleagues would also realise practically and metaphorically that success is built on the sum of the parts being greater than the whole. As an LGBTQ+ female leader, I faced challenging decisions regarding individuals within the group (Tuckman, 2010). My role as a leader was to facilitate discussions about these challenges and explore how our different perspectives and beliefs could align.

In my leadership roles as an LGBTQ+ member of staff I still appreciated that on occasions I would have to wear a mask that made other people feel more comfortable but overtime this strategy became far less called upon; I kept true to the belief that if you simplify the basic characteristics that academic leadership and Sport hold in isolation, key comparable components rise to the surface.

I could cherry-pick from my past work (in schools and athleticism), and I felt that I had developed overtime, the dexterity to navigate priorities into new performance targets, but I often felt undermined by strong members of departments. Like many performers I know that there would be a great deal of trial and error, hence, my strategy was to ensure that all experiences would be reflectively considered as a learning process for the whole team where success and failure was shared.

My life, my past leadership and my commitment to be resilient was never covertly hidden but in conjunction to this reality I did not attend all the official events with my plus one, but I did have a picture of them on my desk and spoke about them like every other member of staff. This was not false, but what I did from the start of my time was try at all costs to make the environment I was working in more familiar. I needed to deliberately get closer to how the people and the internal patterns were working meaning it was less about the functional processes at the start of each of my leadership roles and far more about knowing who I was leading and what their characters were. It was to find out about the hidden secrets and agendas, and by doing so my aim was to reduce as many unknowns as I possibly could so that others could perform well in that environment. Experiences had taught me to prepare for what you can control and not to focus on things that you cannot control.

I needed to know if there were covert homophobic, sexist, racist individuals within the teams that I was leading and the easiest way of acquiring this knowledge was designing parts of the programme content through social justice issues. Individual responses and enthusiasm particularly when challenging heteronormative cultural states told me a great deal about colleagues and learners, and what their priorities and ideologies were.

I wanted to shape the cultural environment that I was leading not just imitating behaviours that had heteronormatively as the dominant force within this paradigm. This was achieved by not continually betraying my authentic self, but subtle changes began to infiltrate the current cultures in play (Darwin, 2000). Throughout my professional and personal life, I have always had a sense of purpose, and morally as an educationalist the way we think and the way we act is unmeasurably washed over those that we encounter.

This was not just because it remained important to me to do so but in education we do not exist in a vacuum, and I wanted colleagues to not only see this within me but also visualise what their actions and behaviours were potentially affording the individuals around them (Freire, 2000). As a female LGBTQ+ individual I wanted to show that colleagues had to appreciate potentially new and adaptive ways that may challenge the current status quo. The truths was, however that on occasions, mimicking aspects of current dominant discourses and selecting traditional strategies was the best way of crafting the cultures I sought. At times compromises did fuel the creation of new environments which afforded myself and others more authentic spaces (Darwin, 2000). I have learnt to comprehend what these working realties were and manage the ever-changing situational inter-plays between 'I as a leader' and 'I as a LGBTQ+ female' these versions of me could and would affect the quality and relationship of 'performance' I had with all of those I worked with.

This chapter has traced my nuanced journey of navigating leadership in the fields of PESSD and higher education. Drawing on decades of experience in teaching and elite sport, it highlights how authenticity, reflexivity and resilience are central to my inclusive leadership. Despite facing structural and cultural barriers, the narrative affirms that leadership grounded in equity and lived experience can shift institutional cultures and inspire the next generation of educators. In reimagining leadership through the lens of social justice, I stress the importance of visibility, community and transformation in shaping more inclusive and empowering educational environments.

REFERENCES

Bushell-Thornalley, H. (2025). Navigating the ethics application process. In A. Brett & C. Lee (Eds.), *The guide to LGBTQ+ research* (1st ed.). Emerald Publishing.

Darwin, C. (2000). *The descent of man, and selection in relation to sex*. Project Gutenberg. http://www.gutenberg.org/ebooks/2300

Foucault, M. (1980). *Power/Knowledge: Selected interviews and other writings, 1972–1977*. Vintage.

Freire, P. (2000). *Pedagogy of the oppressed*. Continuum International Publishing.

Fullan, M. (2016). *The NEW meaning of educational change* (5th ed.). Teachers College Press.

Lee, C. (2023). How do male and female headteachers evaluate their authenticity as school leaders? *Management in Education*, *37*(1), 46–55. https://doi.org/10.1177/0892020621999675

Morley, L. (2013). The rules of the game: Women and the leaderist turn in higher education. *Gender and Education*, *25*(1), 116–131. https://doi.org/10.1080/09540253.2012.740888

Tuckman, B. W. (2010). Leadership teams: Developing and sustaining high performance. *Management Decision*, *48*(2), 340–344. https://doi.org/10.1108/00251741011022653

Section 4

TRANSFORMING LGBTQ+ LEADERSHIP: SYSTEMS, STRUCTURES AND COMMUNITY

14

FOLLOW THE LEADER? CRITICALLY QUESTIONING LGBT+ LEADERSHIP IN THE SURVEILLANCE UNIVERSITY

PIPPA STERK

Kings College London, UK

Keywords: LGBTQ+ leadership; surveillance in higher education; queer pedagogy; authenticity and power; non-performative diversity; LGBTQ+ identities

INTRODUCTION

When I was asked to contribute a chapter on leadership, I wasn't really sure how to respond. I was flattered that someone thought I had worthwhile contributions to make, given that my job might not readily be recognised as a typical 'leadership' position. I was also delighted for my writing to be included among scholars whom I respect so greatly, and from whom I have learnt so much. However, the question of 'leadership' troubles me deeply. Through reflecting on my own teaching experiences, this chapter will explore the tensions and complexities that come with thinking of teaching through a leadership lens. It is both discomfort with leadership, and an inconsistent relationship *to* discomfort, that I want to unpack, though it is not my intent to resolve it.

The tension in this discomfort partially arises because I do not think of myself as a 'leader', and I don't know if I *want* to think of myself as a leader. As a label, it is very unclear, yet it carries so much baggage with it, so many presumptions. At times its lack of clarity is what allows it to carry these presumptions unquestioned: after all, 'leadership' derives its power from being associated with merit. If we are leading something, it is assumed that somehow, we *deserve* to be leaders, since leadership requires a certain level of social recognition and consent from the group that is being led.

Leadership qualities are socially stratified, and differences in our ability to practice leadership skills, but also to be *understood* as leaders, are socially reproduced. If you 'look like a leader' or 'act like a leader' you are more likely to be interpreted as a leader, and to boost your leadership credentials. If we imagine 'leaders' to be white, male, heterosexual, Western and middle-class, then any way in which one does not conform to this archetype, becomes an obstacle to be overcome. The inability or refusal to embody the agreed notion of a leader can suggest that maybe you were never leadership material to begin with. Maybe you don't want it badly enough, maybe you're just not willing to do what it takes.

Because of the hierarchies implicit in the term, I think striving for 'leadership' within LGBT+ contexts can be a bit of a red herring. Yes, there are unequal ways in which leadership gets divided based on who or what is seen as authoritative. But beneath that division is a more urgent question, namely: what do we do with leadership once we get it?

In looking at educational experiences, I refer to Sara Ahmed's concept of the 'non-performative' (Ahmed, 2012).

She draws here on J. L. Austin's performativity theory: the notion that language does not just *describe* the world around us, but can also change this world (Austin, 1962). Ahmed describes how diversity policy and organisational conduct can often be *non*-perfomative. An organisation may make a verbal or written commitment to diversify, but this does not necessarily result in tangible change.

For the purposes of this chapter, I am specifically interested in how this non-performative relationship between the organisation and the communities it serves. In 'Divisions of leadership' I argue that an intent to diversify what leadership looks like, may not actually result in a more diverse attitude towards leadership. Then in 'What are we leading?', I argue that trying to get rid of the authoritarian connotations of leadership does not necessarily make leadership non-hierarchical.

DIVISIONS OF LEADERSHIP

I have taught on a university Bachelor of Arts programme for four years. Every year, during our introduction week over crisps and university-branded wine, I will inevitably be asked at least one of the following questions:

'So what year are you in?'

'Have you been to any Freshers' events?'

'Are you in the morning or the afternoon seminar?'

As I am quite short and dress relatively informally, it is unsurprising that students do not readily interpret me as a member of staff and instead assume that I am one of them. I am also read as a woman (albeit not a conventionally feminine one), I have continued to mask in group settings post-lockdowns, and I am readily racialised as non-white.

Exactly which of these features tips the scale decidedly from 'scholar' to 'student', I will never know for certain.

Usually, within a couple of weeks, as the students and I get to know each other, this corrects itself, and we move on. The course I teach on is heavily influenced by literature on critical pedagogy (Freire, 1996) and aims to foster an egalitarian relationship between teachers and students, challenging normative hierarchies of knowledge and deservingness. I see these 'mistaken identity' interactions as part of this challenge: if I were to dress more 'professionally', would that make my doctorate and university teaching qualification more real? Of course not. Does my skin tone hinder my ability to teach about Bourdieu, Butler, or Baudrillard? Of course it doesn't. So, what is it about the cultural figure of the 'university teacher' that still presumes a certain look? At times, I like embodying this challenge to preconceived notions. Yet, the fact that I cannot opt out of providing this challenge is often uncomfortable knowledge to grapple with.

Given the focus on social justice in our BA degree course the programme generally attracts students who are politically and socially aware. They are interested in exploring issues of inequality and are eager to discuss new ways of approaching and improving the world. However, the desire to reimagine the world takes time to put into practice. In the meantime, those of us who do not fit the traditional ideal of a university teacher are continually made to feel that we add little value to Higher Education.

For example, on an everyday level, although we all encourage students to use our first names rather than titles, male colleagues are still far more likely to be addressed with honorifics than female colleagues. On a structural level, much of the pastoral care and community-building in education continues to fall to women and/or those in precarious academic roles. This is important work, but it is rarely recognised in promotions or job applications, and it often comes at the expense of time for research and publishing.

The specifically 'queer' aspects of my pedagogy and research prioritise slow, communal and interactional forms of learning. These approaches value shared growth over displays of individual intellect (Murphy, 2024). Unfortunately, this is often misunderstood by students and colleagues alike as lacking rigour or skill. Queer pedagogy is sometimes treated as if it requires no expertise, as if anyone could do it, despite it being a field with its own depth, theory and nuance.

Even among colleagues who genuinely want to challenge traditional models of education, there is often a gap between what is said and what is done. Voicing a commitment to change doesn't always translate into changed behaviours or leadership styles. Education should be a space where we keep challenging each other and learning together. But it becomes difficult when the lesson in question is about your own belonging in the academy. That's when the emotional toll sets in.

The struggle to be taken seriously in academia reveals some deep contradictions. We tell our students that looking or sounding clever isn't the same as offering real insight. Yet in academic culture, those who look and sound the part are often the ones most rewarded. We talk about valuing relationships and collective progress, but the system still prioritises research outputs over spending time helping a distressed student.

WHAT ARE WE LEADING?

When we do describe ourselves as leaders within Higher Education, what is it that we imagine ourselves to be leaders of? Higher Education remains a social, financial, and cultural stratifier (Boliver, 2017), and maintains a worldwide colonial hegemony that rewards citizens and scholars in the Global North and systematically devalues and obstructs scholars in the Global South (Albayrak-Aydemir, 2020). Is this a system that we should want to lead? Even if we were to imagine that as individuals, we can make small dents into this system, does it not require *us* to adapt to *it* more than we can ever force *it* to adapt to *us*?

This is another reason why I have difficulty commenting on myself as a leader without further caveats. It reifies educational leadership positions as positions that are desirable and strengthens the paths through which certain people get to be described as leaders – because of course, one only is a leader if others are their followers. In an educational system that is getting more expensive to navigate (Department for Education, 2024) and where jobs are consistently getting cut (UCU Queen Mary, 2024), does an academic position really say as much about your skills and capacities, as it says about your luck and relative privilege. If I am the one who 'made the cut' to have a full-time academic position, that is only because I might have been particularly good at a game that was rigged in my favour to begin with.

Nevertheless, within my academic role, I teach students how to play this game too. As much as wanting to resist educational norms isn't the same as practically resisting these norms, neither does the opening up of 'leadership' empty the concept of its hierarchical effect. For students, I am the everyday face of a system that may decide their future life progression. This is especially so if students are from financially precarious backgrounds or are relatively new to navigating UK education. When a student has less to fall back on, a university degree can make all the more difference to their professional, financial and social circumstances. University degrees can facilitate class mobility, whether we think this is fair or not. No matter the extent to which I would like to reject the power I hold, I cannot deny that it is there.

The power and responsibility that education leaders hold has become more visible recently as suspicion and surveillance of certain student groups has become more overt. It has become commonplace to hear about universities calling the police in response to their own students protesting the genocide in Gaza (Gudge & Mercer-Kelly, 2024; NOS Nieuws, 2024). The recent police violence against student encampments may be a more unapologetic display of institutional power than many are used to, but universities' surveillance of student movement is nothing new. For instance, it has earlier roots in the 'anti-terrorist' Prevent agenda for instance, which became controversial for its potential to infringe on students' privacy (Weale, 2017), and the potential to profile Muslim students and scholars under the guise of safeguarding (National Union of Students, no date). How can we build trust in our classrooms when we represent institutions that increasingly view non-conforming students with suspicion and hostility?

The notion of trust was a constant consideration in writing this chapter - normally, when discussing my own experiences, I would give much more precise and detailed accounts of my interactions. However, when discussing how encounters with students may reinforce normative ideas of teaching and leadership, I decided not to go into specifics. Firstly, this is because I do not want the student-staff interaction to be reduced to potential 'content' in academic writing, or for current and future students to worry that I see them as merely a background character in my individual publishing trajectory.[1]

It is important that I do not fix a student's behaviour in time and place through describing it. The desire to make things permanent, to create a solidified image of a person, is a fundamentally anti-queer one (Halberstam, 2005). What kind of an example would I set, as a reluctant LGBT+

---

[1] For a great consideration of how queer approaches to teaching and learning can become flattened and commercialised through the drive for academic publishing, see (Parker, 2002).

educational leader, if I thought that describing a singular interaction does justice to all the learning my students do?

In an education system increasingly shaped by audits, administration and surveillance, LGBT+ leaders must ask: what exactly are we conforming to when we pursue leadership roles? Of course, it's essential to speak about the homophobia, biphobia and transphobia we experience – both overt and subtle. But we also need to reflect on how our stories might unintentionally reinforce dominant norms.

As marginalised people, we often see our presence in leadership as a form of disruption; a sign of progress from within. And sometimes, it is. But that's not the whole story. If we embrace LGBT+ leadership only as something inherently positive, we risk overlooking the deeper question: what kind of leadership are we participating in, and what are the effects of this leadership?

CONCLUSION

Ultimately, we cannot *will* ourselves out of institutional power. Teacher–student interactions are informed by prior assumptions about hierarchy, both in spite of and because of any marginalised identity we may hold. This means that on one hand we need to constantly, actively challenge how, and to whom we assign intellectual and interpersonal authority. The meaning and the message need to be one here: if we want to instruct students to think differently, we need to encourage them to reflect on how they might reinforce particular ideas about who 'deserves' to be in Higher Education, even if this reflection is uncomfortable.

On the other hand, as LGBT+ teachers we should not act like getting more LGBT+ people in leadership positions destroys these hierarchies. Whilst they may be slightly shifted, they remain largely in place. Refusing to engage with the complexity and contradictions of classroom leadership dynamics is choosing the easy way out. It prevents us from enacting our duty as teacher: to constantly work at making the relationship with our students as meaningful as possible. This includes challenging preconceived notions of social stratification, both in our students and in ourselves. We might get it wrong more often than we get it right, but that shouldn't stop us from trying.

REFERENCES

Ahmed, S. (2012). *On being included: Racism and diversity in institutional life*. Duke University Press.

Albayrak-Aydemir, N. (2020, February 20). The hidden costs of being a scholar from the Global South. *LSE Higher Education*. https://blogs.lse.ac.uk/highereducation/2020/02/20/the-hidden-costs-of-being-a-scholar-from-the-global-south/. Accessed on February 14, 2025

Austin, J. L. (1962). *How to do things with words*. Harvard University Press.

Boliver, V. (2017). Misplaced optimism: How higher education reproduces rather than reduces social inequality. *British Journal of Sociology of Education*, 38(3), 423–432. https://doi.org/10.1080/01425692.2017.1281648

Department for Education. (2024). *Student fees and maintenance loan increase: What you need to know – The Education Hub*. https://educationhub.blog.gov.uk/2024/11/student-fees-and-maintenance-loan-increase-what-you-need-to-know/. Accessed on February 14, 2025

Freire, J. L. (1996). *Pedagogy of the oppressed* (New rev. ed). Penguin Books.

Gudge, E., & Mercer-Kelly, P. (2024). Oxford University Gaza protest sees 16 arrested. *BBC News*. https://www.bbc.com/news/articles/c0ddzejlndvo. Accessed on February 14, 2025

Halberstam, J. (2005). *In a queer time and place: Transgender bodies, subcultural lives*. NYU Press.

Murphy, D. (2024). Accessing a queer pedagogy: Identity, power dynamics, and a queerer form of teaching in higher education. *Postgraduate Pedagogies*, 4(1). https://postgradpedagogies.lse.ac.uk/articles/24. Accessed on February 14, 2025

National Union of Students. (no date). *Prevent @ NUS Connect*. https://www.nusconnect.org.uk/liberation/black-students/anti-racism-and-anti-fascism/prevent. Accessed on February 14, 2025

NOS Nieuws. (2024). *Zes activisten aangehouden op verdenking van vernielingen op Radboud universiteit*. https://nos.nl/artikel/2548605-zes-activisten-aangehouden-op-verdenking-van-vernielingen-op-radboud-universiteit. Accessed on February 14, 2025

Parker, M. (2002). Queering management and organization. *Gender, Work and Organization*, 9(2), 146–166. https://doi.org/10.1111/1468-0432.00153

UCU Queen Mary. (2024, March 23). *UK HE shrinking*. https://qmucu.org/qmul-transformation/uk-he-shrinking/. Accessed on February 14, 2025

Weale, S. (2017, January 20). London University tells students their emails may be monitored. *The Guardian*. https://www.theguardian.com/uk-news/2017/jan/20/university-warns-students-emails-may-be-monitored-kings-college-london-prevent. Accessed on February 14, 2025

15

LESSONS LEARNT BECOMING UCL IOE'S FIRST AND ONLY

SIMON LIU

University College London, UK

INTRODUCTION

Before becoming part of the world of Higher Education Institution (HEI) Diversity, Equality, and Inclusion (DEI), you could summarise me professionally as: TEFL teacher—Teacher of English as a Foreign Language. I am very proud of these two words, but they exist very much isolated from the world of DEI in HEIs. However, what you will find in this chapter is that I (intentionally) stumbled into DEI as I did with teaching and like with teaching, I have not left the rabbit hole since, nor do I want to. I am hoping that, by sharing my journey towards my LGBTQ+ equity position and work, you will be able to see more of your own roadmap towards contributing to LGBTQ+ educational leadership; you will find your own way towards helping our LGBTQ+ community rise in any sector, department, group or HEI context that you are a part of.

Simon Liu

Leading a Classroom vs Leading for a Community

In the Spring of 2005, I remember seeing an advert in my university for a certified initial teacher training course to become an English as a Foreign Language teacher. I do not remember the details. I do not even remember if it was a paper (yes, paper) or digital advert (as they both existed back then). I just remembered that I knew that teaching was what I wanted to do for the rest of my working life.

With hindsight, I can now really see so many similarities and crossovers between teaching a class and promoting DEI. TEFL teachers seek to actively bring out, raise and platform all voices, especially the quietest ((British Council, n.d.); (BALEAP, 2022); (Bakogiannis, 2024)); we seek to develop everyone's ability to understand as well as be understood by others ((British Council, n.d.); (BALEAP, 2022); (Bakogiannis, 2024)); we literally equip everyone with language as a tool and develop everyone's ability to use their tool to speak their truths (British Council, n.d.); our success is measured in how much everyone is able to tell us their stories and how much we can understand them.

Moreover, sadly and indignantly, I also saw my own marginalised identities ignored, prejudiced and/or even burdening throughout my career, personally sensitising me to the inequalities in a seemingly open, benevolent and multicultural industry. In my experience, I had never seen open formal acceptance for LGBTQ+ people (Bollas, 2024, as cited in Hunter, 2024); thus my sexuality was always an additional factor that I had to decide whether to disclose along with any potential consequences. My race—my Chinese heritage ethnicity—had always been on my mind when an application was ignored or an interview not offered despite my sizeable teaching qualifications and experience; there has always been an extra pressure and implied expectation that I have to prove my English is as good if not better than a non-person of colour despite being born and raised in Scotland (Savski, 2021). Moreover, my mental health condition—Generalised Anxiety Disorder (G.A.D)—had always felt like my problem to perfectly communicate, accommodate with others and made others uncomfortable to know. Fortunately, my teaching, then later my DEI work, became a vehicle by which I could platform the marginalised voices of others when mine might not have always been; I appreciated the sense of justice that I could bring to others.

Long before I had even heard of DEI, I was already aware of the practice of platforming equality, understanding the value of diversity as well as how lack of inclusion is simply exclusion; moreover, I had also had unfortunate experiences on an intersectional level with my multiple marginalised identities. It really does not take too much to see why equity work opportunities would start to appeal to me when they appeared.

UNDERSTANDING YOUR ORGANISATION

In the January of 2021, I remember seeing a recruitment announcement for my faculty's Athena SWAN Silver Award Self-assessment Team. I do not remember the details. I remember it was digital (because it was 2021). But I also remember this part of it: 'We particularly encourage applications from *LGBTQ+ staff, disabled staff and male staff,* who are currently under-represented as highlighted within the Bronze Award Action Plan'. This meant in an instant that DEI was something that I knew I wanted to be part of, potentially for the rest of my working life. The only thing is—I had no idea how to do any of it. Although I had waxed lyrical about the similarities between teaching and DEI in the previous section, it was only after years of doing DEI work that I could reflect and notice these overlapping features. The first thing that you learn about institutional DEI work is that it is... well, institutional. That is to say you need to understand the structure of the organisation before you are really able to make any contribution to its further betterment (Baird & Lee, 2025). I started to build up an internal map of my faculty, as well as how it fit into my university. I realised that we are all very cocooned within our own small group or team, especially in a large organisation such as a university, but there are so many people with interlocking roles and functions that make the organisation run, yet we never really understand who we interlock with. It only dawned on me—much embarrassingly later after joining Athena SWAN—how institutional change requires understanding institutional mechanisms (Baird & Lee, 2025).

The next major lesson was about finding out the obscure inequalities beneath your own organisation's bold and noteworthy achievements and marketable presentation. At the time (and true now), I felt that my workplace had the best working conditions and colleagues that I had ever experienced. But what I learnt from conversations with Athena SWAN colleagues, and empirical and qualitative data gathering exercises such as surveys and focus group interviews was that disadvantaged experiences are hidden, perhaps even invisible... unless actively sought (Belkin et al., 2024). These individuals contribute just as much to your organisation's prestige—in fact, I would argue in some ways more perhaps because they must when they feel so much more is being asked of them ((Williamson et al., 2021; Betancourt et al., 2024)). I will illustrate with personal examples to avoid disclosing others' experiences: as an LGBTQ+ individual with Chinese heritage and a mental health condition, when I *have to* speak more assertively, write more clearly and intellectually and teach more impactfully than a non-person of colour—these are not equal expectations nor equal teaching work. When I *have to* decide with each interaction if the other person will treat me differently because of my sexuality, my professional relationships are not formed on equal terms to those who do not. When I *have to* make all arrangements and accommodations to fit my mental health requirements to a non-G.A.D-sufferer's working pattern, I *have to* disadvantage my life to advantage the preferred schedule of others. Yet, I was still shocked to find out the underlying inequalities even though I had hidden, diminished, dismissed and ignored them all throughout my working career. As with others, I did not look beneath the surface (Strebler & O'Regan, 2005) and assumed I was the only one experiencing these unequal experiences.

It is only when I started to grasp both the workings of my institution and started to perceive the almost undetectable experiences of inequality that I was able to start to find out what I could do to contribute to a better organisation.

DEVELOPING DEI LEADERSHIP SKILLS

Now, it is all fine and well to have this heightened awareness of both organisational structure as well as inequalities, but it is also quite another to be able to carry out meaningful activity leading to change. This is where I learnt to observe, admire and learn from the successful DEI practitioners around me—all while drawing inspiration from the persons themselves and how they practise. Once again, I will draw a comparison to how I learnt DEI from my first career: Teachers are exposed to quite complex learning theories along with comprehensive lesson plans or models before they are to observe practice of those models and consideration of those theories by other more experienced teachers during real lessons. It is not through the direct mimicry or emulation of another teacher's exact lesson that teachers become good at their craft; it is through the reflection on their own practice after each and every lesson time and time again that leads to them planning, practising and responding more and more effectively i.e. nurturing a specific group of individuals who need your help to grow ((Farrell, 2020; Mann & Walsh, 2017)). I have found myself doing just that from observing DEI practice around me. By far, the thing which is easiest to relate to DEI from teaching is delivering workshops. Once I became aware of the underlying inequity or bias being focused on in an DEI workshop, I was able to very easily see the order and purpose of all the activities that stemmed from it—as I would from a lesson. I then understood the positive intentionality-setting at the beginning of a workshop, the open engaging conversations to relate participants' experiences and perceptions with the key themes and of course the specific recommendations for next steps to learn and do more to address inequality or bias in question. When, for instance, one considers the lack of awareness surrounding LGBTQ+ staff members' complicated decision-making in disclosure or non-disclosure of their sexuality or gender identity (Tate & Glazzard, 2024), I was able to plan a workshop like a lesson on engaging participants to consider and empathise with the different factors that need to be considered before an LGBTQ+ person feels safe revealing their sexuality or gender identity.

What I found surprisingly intuitive to learn but is often extremely difficult to carry out in real-life was how to bring a group together to collaboratively work towards structural and institutional change. From observing activities during my time in my faculty's Athena SWAN group, I saw that it was not easy for the Chair to single-handedly bring together a large (and later I found out ever-changing) cohort of unconnected individuals throughout one of my university's largest faculties by staff or student number to bring about institutional change for all those who felt marginalised. I noted that recruiting those with a strong genuine interest as a key—given that any DEI work involves contributions from many, this was an engrained lesson that would benefit me in the formation of my own advisory group. From my experience on the faculty Athena SWAN team, I also saw that consistently sharing the group's meaningful purpose and what each group member's function or contribution was also an important element in successfully collectivising collaborative efforts. Importantly alongside this, it is also crucial to understand that voluntary contributions and participation require accommodation, understanding and flexibility from the group's leader as such group members are *choosing* to work *with* you, not *having to* work *for* you: 'effective leaders influence others to accomplish goals' (Lee, 2021, p. 92).

I observed, admired and reflected on how the Athena SWAN group was organised and managed to eventual Silver Award success for the faculty. But, more importantly, as with learning from the workshop – to me another teacher's lesson, I reflected on how it could change my own practice in my own particular context in order to meet the challenge of being the IOE's first and only to date Faculty LGBTQ+ Equity Lead.

LEARN CONTINUALLY

If I had to summarise the key tenets of LGBTQ+ equity success from my experience, I would say never stop learning about 'policy, procedure and professional relationships'. Based on these three cornerstones—or guiding principles, I have found that I could enact meaningful change for the LGBTQ+ community in my faculty which had never existed before, even when it did not seem like there was a clear path to doing this.

First off, it might seem inattentive (or even remiss) of me to not discuss in depth the sheer amount of fine and nuanced understanding of the LGBTQ+ community; the range of sexual and gender identities; the experiences of marginalisation; the overwhelming media and public misinterpretation and misrepresentation and, of course, famously, terminology of the community that are all required of someone in my role. I suppose I will need to draw another comparison between DEI and teaching here: What sets a queer DEI practitioner apart from a queer academic is not just what they know, but how they use that knowledge to make a difference in people's lives.

From my experience over the past four or more years effecting change for my faculty and university, I think that intimate knowledge of 'policy' has been one of my most effective tools for effecting said change. You might be thinking 'hold on, this doesn't sound very inspirational or awe-affirming' – sifting through masses of text about central university HR guidance; navigating labyrinthine webpages across the central university hub, faculty-specific and individual departmental/division websites; staring at dozens of institutional rules on seemingly each and every type of activity that could take place, *but that* is how you learn how to make things happen which have never happened before.

Embracing being a student of organisational policy could be one of the most valuable decisions you ever make in this role.

It is only when you are able to grasp your institution's policy structure for the respective area in which you wish to make change that you can then move onto the next essential tool for change: 'procedure'. A key example of this is creating a dedicated website for the LGBTQ+ community within your faculty's intranet system. You cannot simply look up how to create a SharePoint site on YouTube then add it as you wish onto your faculty's website. Instead, you would need to understand how the intranet system is managed, edited and overseen by the appointed team e.g. Marketing and Communications. From there, you would need to decide the content which is in reference to your institution's official relevant *policy*. This is not even including learning the capabilities of a SharePoint site, the exact engagement style with your community or even how to get this signed off by the appropriate persons in charge. No, that would then turn to the dynamics of 'professional relationships' within the institution.

In addition to, essentially, understanding the rulebook and playbook on how to play (queer) ball in your organisation, you also need to work with the key players on the field with you. The most precious resource here is 'goodwill'—showing it, perceiving it, receiving it, exchanging it and, most importantly, *creating* it. You can honestly never overvalue it, and you can never really stop learning how it contributes to furthering equity in your institution. I am sure that there has been a plethora of ways of going about this, but I can only speak for myself in this chapter: I stick to my personal principles of 'clear positive vision' and 'personable good faith communication'.

When I say, 'clear positive vision', hopefully that will resonate with you in the sense that one would most likely have plans, ideas, events, activities, changes or even simply just suggestions when wanting to embark on LGBTQ+ leadership in HEI—or DEI in any organisation. These thoughts of yours are *not* obvious, nor perhaps have ever occurred to the key stakeholders in your context—especially non-LGBTQ+ stakeholders. This then therefore involves a process of learning to translate your 'vision' into specific concrete ideas that fit your organisation's *policy* and *procedure*. You should consider questions such as: What exact event, activity or change do I want to enact e.g. an LGBTQ+ informational website? How can I explain the need and impact to the (non-LGBTQ+) stakeholders involved? Am I aware of the exact procedural steps needed to make this happen?

My other personal principle is practising 'personable good faith relationships' whenever communicating with others in your equity role; in short, this just means forming a trusting one-on-one relationship based on positive intentionality with whomever you come across. In practice, this means remembering small things colleagues have told you e.g. holiday plans or sharing small things about yourself e.g. a love for sci-fi/fantasy movies; or even just remembering to show appreciation for a prompt or helpful email response. On the occasion when these interactions may seem not to bear fruit, it is worth remembering that you are not alone, and that there are others who have struggled with this—such as LGBTQ+ presidents (Gonzalez, 2024). Draw on conversations with others in your workplace or any queer networks which you are a part of—you are unlikely to be the only one experiencing this. But also, remember, over time, with each and every communication, you accumulate a sense of positive anticipation and a willingness to help which can only grow as goodwill within your organisation.

CONCLUSION

To leave a parting message of hope and, hopefully, inspiration, you will find your way if you really want to help your organisation become a fairer, more welcoming and integrated place for its LGBTQ+ community. From my experience of developing LGBTQ+ leadership in my faculty, you should first draw on your lived experiences as a queer person to help you gain an LGBTQ+ perspective of your organisation—further reflecting on any potential intersectional experiences such as race or disability can only empower you to see the change that needs to take place. Even developing a clearer awareness of how your marginalised identity has affected your day-to-life in your workplace e.g. deciding to (not) come out to different colleagues provides the understanding to pursue policy change. Non-LGBTQ+ stakeholders in particular will turn to you for your awareness of the community's lived experiences and perspective which you can use to advocate for specific changes e.g. an informational LGBTQ+-specific website.

I would then say to find connections between what you know how to do and —such as, with myself, teaching a lesson and delivering a workshop. A good way to find out how you can contribute to DEI is by joining an established group or award scheme dedicated to DEI e.g. Advance HE—Athena SWAN. You may find that you already have transferable skills or knowledge that can help you effect change as an LGBTQ+ leader. If not, it is a very good place to learn from others' experience to develop a necessary skillset or knowledge. From my own experience being part of an Athena SWAN self-assessment team, I observed first-hand that equity leadership involves inspiring others through communicating and inviting others to collaborate on focussed beneficial outcomes for your community.

Once again, I would reiterate 'policy' and 'procedure'. Once you have developed your version of a 'clear positive vision' for your organisation, invest your time into finding out exactly which specific websites, documents or contact persons will help you make that particular project, event or activity a reality. Although initially unexciting and seemingly fruitless trying to digest a large amount of institutional information, you will find that this very information is exactly what you need to make what you envision come to life.

Finally, do not underestimate the power of your professional relationships built on good faith and goodwill. You will rarely find yourself in a situation where you alone enact a meaningful change for your community; instead, you are more likely to find that you will accomplish the most by leading a vision and others to follow it with you.

REFERENCES

Baird, A., & Lee, C. (2025). A blueprint for LGBTQ+ leadership development in UK higher education. *Management in Education*, 0(0). https://doi.org/10.1177/08920206251330424

Bakogiannis, A. (2024). Exploring inclusive teaching practices of English for academic purposes (EAP) in higher education (HE): A call for systemic change. *Journal of Learning Development in Higher Education*, 31. [Preprint]. https://doi.org/10.47408/jldhe.vi31.1282

BALEAP. (2022). Our EDI statement. *BALEAP Values and EDI Statement*. https://www.baleap.org/values-and-edi-statement

Belkin, L., Lander, A., & McCormack, M. (2024). Impossible visibilities of Black and Global Majority staff at an ethnically diverse English university. *International Journal of Qualitative Studies in Education*, *38*(1), 1–16. https://doi.org/10.1080/09518398.2024.2348812

Betancourt, R. M., Baluchi D, D., K., Campbell, K. M., & Rodríguez, J. E. (2024). Minority tax on medical students: A review of the literature and mitigation recommendations. *Family Medicine*, *56*(3), 169–175. https://doi.org/10.22454/FamMed.2024.268466

Bollas, A. (2024). LGBTQI+ sexualities and a diversity-focused approach in English for academic purposes. In A.-M. Hunter (Ed.), *Diversity and inclusion in English language education – supporting learning through research and practice* (pp. 103–116). Routledge. https://doi.org/10.4324/9781003258865

British Council. (n.d.). *Using inclusive practices*. Teaching English. https://www.teachingenglish.org.uk/professional-development/teachers/inclusive-practices

Farrell, T. S. C. (2020). *Reflective teaching, revised*. TESOL International Association. https://doi.org/10.4324/9781003178729

Gonzalez, A. J. (2024). *Voices from the field 2024: LGBTQ+ presidents in higher education*. The TIAA Institute. American Council on Education. https://www.acenet.edu/Documents/Voices-From-The-Field-LGBTQ-Presidents-2024.pdf

Lee, C. (2021). Promoting diversity in university leadership: The argument for LGBTQ+ specific leadership programmes in higher education. *Perspectives (Association of University Administrators (U.K.)) Policy and Practice in Higher Education*, 25(3), 91–99. https://doi.org/10.1080/13603108.2021.1877205

Mann, S., & Walsh, S. (2017). *Reflective practice in English language teaching – research-based principles and practices*. Routledge. https://doi.org/10.4324/9781315733395

Savski, K. (2021). Dialogicality and racialized discourse in TESOL recruitment. *Tesol Quarterly*, 55(3), 795–816. https://doi.org/10.1002/tesq.3013

Strebler, M., & O'Regan, S. (2005). *Non-disclosure and hidden discrimination in higher education*. Institute of Employment Studies. https://www.employment-studies.co.uk/system/files/resources/files/424.pdf

Tate, A., & Glazzard, J. (2024). Including LGBTQ+ early career higher education staff: Learning from the policy and practice for supporting LGBTQ+ students. *Higher Education Research and Development*, 44(2), 299–306. https://doi.org/10.1080/07294360.2024.2393117

Williamson, T., Goodwin, C. R., & Ubel, P. A. (2021). Avoiding overtaxing minorities when we need them most. *New England Journal of Medicine*, 384(20), 1877–1879. https://www.nejm.org/doi/10.1056/NEJMp2100179

16

LEAVING TO LEAD: REIMAGINING INCLUSION IN HIGHER EDUCATION AS A BLACK, NEURODIVERGENT, LESBIAN LEADER

CATHERINE MILLAN

Be What You See Consultancy, UK

MY BACKGROUND

At 14, I became a carer, already navigating responsibilities beyond my years while carrying the weight of feeling different. It was not just my race or home life; it was the discomfort I felt with gendered stereotypes forced on me. I grew up in a world that told me in loud, subtle and constant ways that being heterosexual was the only acceptable way to exist. Anything outside of that was wrong. Shameful. Something to be hidden or fixed. From the playground to the classroom, to the media I consumed, heterosexuality was the norm; it was the only option ever presented as acceptable. I knew from an incredibly youthful age that I did not fit into that box. I grew up unable to fully express my masculine gender expression and sexual orientation, not just because of pressure from my peers but out of fear of discrimination from teachers and even family members. I was told constantly, 'You're such a tomboy' or 'She'll grow out of it', which left me feeling even more confused. In school, we learnt what was on the curriculum, but that curriculum never reflected my reality. There was no space for conversations about sexuality, about gender expression or about difference. My culture, my questions, my queerness, none of it existed in the books we read, the lessons taught or the examples given. That erasure left me spending most of my teenage years masking, hiding and trying to blend in, even when it was eating me up inside.

VISIBILITY AS RESISTANCE

Even though the Equality Act came into force in 2010, legal protection does not automatically change hearts and minds. While progress was made on paper, the word 'lesbian' was still used as an insult in corridors and classrooms. It carried judgement and shame, and even now, I sometimes hesitate to say it aloud when describing my own identity. Years of internalised fear and hearing it weaponised against me is something I am still unlearning. But that discrimination also lit a fire in me. It sparked a passion for changing education. At Leeds Beckett University, I gained the language to understand the system—not just what we teach but how and why. I did not want to just teach the curriculum; I wanted to lead it. I wanted to help reimagine the systems: to shape inclusive curricula, reform school processes and make sure future generations did not grow up with the same kind of erasure I did. Education became my lens for change, and I started to see leadership as a way of rewriting the script.

University was also where I began to fully embrace my identity. I found my community a group of brilliant, open, supportive women, and over those years, I learnt how to feel comfortable and accept my sexuality. For the first time, I felt safe being 'out'. I felt seen, and I started to believe that my identity was not a barrier to leadership; it was a source of strength. Freedom did not last. In my final year, I was the victim of a vicious, racial and homophobic attack by a group of men. Several of my friends and I ended up in hospital. The trauma left deep emotional scars ones I carried for years. It shook me to my core. After that, everything changed. I began to retreat. I no longer felt safe expressing who I really was. Public displays of affection became a risk I was not willing to take. I constantly scanned rooms, measuring whether it was safe to mention my sexuality. I had spent years building confidence in my identity, and in one night, that progress was ripped away. I started hiding again, shrinking parts of myself to survive.

The attack did not just affect my sense of safety; it disrupted my sense of leadership. I had started to see myself as someone who could lead authentically, someone who could use their identity as a source of empathy, insight and connection. However, after that night, I no longer felt like I could bring my whole self into any space. For years of my early career, I had to choose between being visible and being safe. The everyday homophobia I faced at work was relentless, often disguised as jokes or curiosity. Comments like 'You just haven't met the right man' or 'What a waste' were common, and over time, chipped away at my psychological safety. Nevertheless, beneath the ignorance was a lack of understanding and empathy. I held onto the belief that education was the most powerful tool to change that. Lesbian women often face a double burden of gender and sexuality-based microaggressions at work. A report of 'Women in the Workplace 2024' found that 71% of women experience microaggressions, with many feeling unable to talk openly about their personal lives. These repeated slights have a cumulative effect, lesbian women who face them are three times more likely to consider leaving their jobs (Lean In and McKinsey & Company, 2018).

In 2017, after years working across global education and humanitarian sectors, training teachers, supporting girls back into school and embedding inclusive curriculum practices, I joined the University of Manchester, ready to bring that experience into UK higher education. I was excited to start my new role, focused on student recruitment and success. My work centred on supporting students from the global majority and delivering training to staff about the systemic barriers these students face within higher education. I was especially passionate about bringing an intersectional lens to this work, ensuring that the voices and experiences of LGBTQ+ students from the global majority were not overlooked but centred in conversations about equity and inclusion.

REWRITING THE RULES OF LEADERSHIP

Moving to Manchester felt like a fresh start. The city's visible queer inclusivity from LGBTQ+ bookshops to Pride flags in windows gave me hope that I would not have to hide who I was, but on my first day at the university, I hesitated. Faced with the question about sexual orientation on my induction form, I could not bring myself to tick 'lesbian'. I was out in my personal life, but I was not sure it was safe in my working life. I am not alone. The Pride In Leadership report: Barriers to LGBTQ+ career progression in the United Kingdom (Ebrey & Haworth, 2025) shows 30% of participants have never come out to customers or clients, often due to fear of discrimination or reputational impact and 40% of those who came out after age 35 felt the timing had negatively impacted their career trajectory.

The weeks that followed, I quietly searched for answers by attending staff events, network meetings and looking for signs of inclusion. At one LGBTQ+ staff meeting, I was to find I was the only Black women in a room of 30. In a university with 13,000 staff, could I really be the only lesbian of colour? It left me feeling both hyper-visible and completely unseen.

After connecting with the Diversity, Equality and Inclusion (DEI) team and expressing my passion for enhancing LGBTQ+ inclusion, I was invited to speak at my first ALL-OUT Allies workshop. This initiative focuses on staff members who actively support LGBTQ+ equality in the workplace by demonstrating visible support, engaging with resources and promoting an inclusive culture throughout the university. I loved the concept. It was about shifting the burden, moving away from expecting marginalised communities to fix the problems they did not create, and instead equipping others to take responsibility. Standing in front of that room, sharing my coming-out story with a group of staff I had never met, was a defining moment. It was not just about educating; it was about embracing my visibility as an LGBTQ+ leader. Even though the audience had not lived my experience, I could see them leaning in, listening and connecting. There was something powerful about watching empathy take root, knowing that by owning my truth, I was helping create safer, more inclusive spaces for others, too.

A few months into my role, the Manchester Arena attack shook the city. While Manchester responded with public unity, tensions and hate crimes, particularly racism and Islamophobia, rose sharply in the aftermath. As a Black lesbian, I felt increasingly exposed. Racial microaggressions became more frequent, often accompanied by comments that targeted my sexuality. It was a stark reminder of how layered discrimination can be and how urgently it needs to be addressed. This period pushed me to step more fully into my leadership. I approached the university with a proposal to tackle rising hate through education and was supported with funding to develop a workplace discrimination prevention training programme, which became 'The Diversity Champions Project' (EDI Champions, 2025). It was a turning point not just in my career but in realising that leadership meant using my voice to drive structural change in moments of crisis.

The Diversity Champions Project trained staff, students, local school pupils and teachers on anti-racism, gender equity, LGBTQ+ inclusion, ableism and neurodiversity, all underpinned by practical *Active Bystander Intervention* training. Participants then engaged in a 'train the trainer' model, developing their own workshops to deliver and cascade change within their schools, teams and student groups. The programme led me to research and explore *Active Bystander theory* in more depth. Rooted in social psychology, it empowers individuals to safely intervene when they witness harm (Latané & Darley, 1970). Studies show that such interventions are effective in addressing everyday discrimination, particularly in educational and workplace settings (Burn, 2009; Katz et al., 2011).

During this time, I had the chance to work with Catherine Prescott from the DEI team, who had launched the 'Speak Up, Stand Up' campaign part of the Diversity and Inclusion Student Ambassador project (Office for Student n.d). Collaborating with her was inspiring; she was a visionary leader and closely guided me on how to expand the Diversity Champions programme, which led to me securing £10,000 from the university's Investing in Success grant. This was a pivotal leadership moment. Within the first few years, the Diversity Champions programme led to fewer incidents of racism and homophobia in schools, and pupils grew more confident using bystander techniques. It also contributed to staff development and strengthened the university's submissions for the Stonewall Equality Index and Race Equality Charter Mark.

FROM ERASURE TO IMPACT

By the third year, it had gained real traction across the city and sector. It was recognised with numerous awards, including *The Spirit of Manchester Award*, *The Outstanding Social Behavioural Change Award* and a *Making a Difference Award* from the University of Manchester. I also received a personal *Outstanding Contribution Award* from Dame Nancy Rothwell. These were more than achievements. They were moments of transformation. I was no longer just delivering a project. I was leading a movement. I had begun to see myself as a leader, someone not only capable of identifying systemic problems but also full of innovative, practical solutions to address them. The more I understood about the structures within higher education, the clearer it became; if we want systems to serve everyone, we need leaders who reflect the communities they aim to support, and I was already one of them.

I joined the Stonewall Award Committee as a volunteer, and it was here I was given the opportunity to examine LGBTQ+ inclusion through systems, processes and cultural change. I became part of a team working to implement meaningful changes across the university, not just to address overt discrimination but also to tackle the deeper, systemic issues embedded in processes and structures. My specific area of focus was external engagement and service delivery. I was responsible for reporting on how the university was improving engagement both internally and externally. Through this work, I began to see the impact the university was having on LGBTQ+ communities beyond its employees.

Through all of this, something unexpected started to happen. I no longer shied away from being seen I started becoming more comfortable with being visible, being viewed as not just a leader but a LGBTQ+ leader. For so long, I had associated visibility with risk, but now I was learning to associate it with impact. I realised that by standing in my truth, I could create space for others to do the same. Within my first year on the Stonewall Award committee, I supported the *Colours Youth Festival* taking place at the University of Manchester, which was run by LGBTQ+ people from the global majority. *Colours* were formerly a national network that created spaces for young LGBTQ+ people from the global majority to connect, build support networks and celebrate their identities. Bringing this festival to Manchester felt powerful. After growing up with little LGBTQ+ representation and no inclusive education, this was another opportunity to support positive change for the next generation. A chance to create the kind of space I once needed.

Working on the Colours Youth Festival project reminded me that leadership is not just about presence, it is about advocacy. It is about making sure those who do not yet have a seat at the table are still heard, valued and included. This was a moment where I was helping to shape long-term, generational change. Through the EDI Champions Programme and my work on the Stonewall Committee, I was finally achieving what I had set out to do. Transforming education systems to be more inclusive, equitable and representative. This felt like a defining moment. These were not just projects they were shifting culture, and I was part of that change. Then the pandemic hit and everything changed. The EDI Champions project was paused, community work cancelled and I found myself behind a laptop for seven hours a day, five days a week. The connection, energy and purpose I had built my role around disappeared, and I began to struggle.

During COVID, I returned to study and was soon diagnosed with attention-deficit/hyperactivity disorder (ADHD) and dyslexia. It felt like coming out all over again this time as neurodivergent. The process was familiar and once again, I was navigating systems not built for people like me.

Instead of holding me back, this new layer of identity strengthened my commitment to inclusive leadership. At this time, I submitted a proposal to make the Diversity Champions Programme my full-time role to scale its impact and embed inclusion into the university's fabric. Despite clear outcomes and growing demand, the proposal was rejected. I was at a crossroads. Leadership often entails seeing beyond what others are ready to act on. The programme was not just training; it was the cultural infrastructure higher education desperately needed. When faced with a 'no,' I realised I did not need permission to lead. So, I left.

I took the leap and started my own business, *Be What You See Consultancy* (Be What You See Consultancy Ltd, 2022), *a workplace discrimination prevention training company*. The name reflected a truth I had carried my whole life: '*You can't be what you can't see.*' Growing up without role models, I wanted to create visibility not just for myself but for every person who had ever been made to feel unseen. My mission was to expand the workplace discrimination prevention training and help drive cultural change across the sector. Within four months, I was fully booked. Not long after, the university invited me back, this time to deliver the same training I had once proposed, now through my own business. It was a full-circle moment, a quiet validation and proof that sometimes leadership means stepping out first, even when others are not ready to follow. What started as a one-woman initiative is now a growing team of over 10 people; our clients include universities, NHS trusts and even a Premier League football club. Every training day, every conversation reinforces my commitment to meaningful inclusion. Teaching people how to recognise and challenge workplace discrimination is not just training to me; it is legacy work and I carry that responsibility with pride and purpose. While writing this chapter, I was awarded the Northern Power Women 'Person with Purpose' Award. Standing on that stage, I felt something shift. I was proud not just of the journey but of who I am: a Black, female, neurodivergent lesbian. In that moment, it felt as though others now recognised me as the leader, I had always known myself to be. Leadership, I have learnt, is not about titles or approval; it is about alignment, action and authenticity. If there is one message, I want to leave you with, it is this:

> *You do not have to wait to be chosen.*
>
> *You can choose yourself. And when you do, you do not just create space, you lead them.*

REFERENCES

Be What You See Consultancy Ltd. (2022). *Be what you see.* https://www.bewhatyousee.co.uk

Burn, S. M. (2009). A situational model of sexual assault prevention through bystander intervention. *Sex Roles*, *60* (11–12), 779–792. https://doi.org/10.1007/s11199-008-9581-5

Ebrey, C., & Haworth, M. (2025). *Barriers to LGBTQ+ career development in the UK: The pride in leadership report*. https://prideinleadership.co.uk/LGBTQ-career-barriers-report-2025

EDI Champions. (2025). *Young persons EDI champion's programme*. https://www.bewhatyousee.co.uk/young-peoples-edi-champions

Katz, J., Heisterkamp, A., & Fleming, W. (2011). The social justice roots of the Mentors in Violence Prevention model and its application in a high school setting. *Violence Against Women*, *17*(6), 684–702. https://doi.org/10.1177/1077801211409725

Latané, B., & Darley, J. M. (1970). *The unresponsive bystander: Why doesn't he help?* Appleton-Century-Crofts.

Lean In and McKinsey and Company. (2018). *Women in the workplace: Everyday discrimination – microaggressions*. https://leanin.org/women-in-the-workplace/2018/everyday-discrimination-microaggressions

17

CONCLUSION

CATHERINE LEE AND DANIEL BURMAN

Anglia Ruskin University, UK

REIMAGINING EDUCATION LEADERSHIP FROM THE MARGINS

This book is a milestone collection of testimonies and reflections from LGBTQ+ educators working across every stage of the UK education system. Spanning early years, primary, secondary, further and higher education, as well as consultancy, research and policy, the chapters in this volume collectively invite a reimagining of what LGBTQ+ leadership means, where it is located and whom it serves. Contributors do not just seek inclusion within existing leadership paradigms. Rather, they offer alternative understandings of leadership, drawn from their own lived experience, and values-led practice. Across the book, leadership emerges not as authority or status but as an ethical, emotionally literate and community-rooted mode of engagement in all phases of Education.

THE ENDURING SHADOW OF SECTION 28

A prominent and persistent theme is the enduring legacy of Section 28. Contributors including Holly Coull, Gerlinde Achenbach, Catherine Lee and Dan Burman. Each illuminate how this legislation shaped a culture of silence that has endured long after its repeal in 2003. Coull's account reveals how its shadow informed the fear and uncertainty she experienced as a school leader in a faith-based setting. Achenbach's memories of navigating school leadership under the active constraints of Section 28 speak to the vigilance, resilience and double lives led by many queer teachers of her generation. Lee and Burman situate Section 28 within a wider social narrative, making clear that for LGBTQ+ people, their leadership skills are often forged and developed in response to adversity, invisibility and erasure.

Although no longer enshrined in law, Section 28's legacy persists. Richard McDonald, Jonny Tridgell and Charlotte Feather highlight how LGBTQ+ educators today still experience hesitation, particularly when contemplating visibility in professional contexts. For many, this manifests as a burden of constant self-regulation and intense emotional labour. Visibility as an LGBTQ+ educator is never neutral. Throughout this book it is shown to be fraught and complex, imbued with risk, reception and self-preservation.

AUTHENTICITY AS LEADERSHIP PRACTICE

Despite its complexity, authenticity emerges as a defining feature of LGBTQ+ leadership in education. And many of our contributors consistently reject simplistic or tokenistic interpretations of authenticity. For Kelsey-Ann Caldow, authenticity is practiced daily through gentle but radical pedagogies in their early years classrooms. Their use of inclusive language, modelling of gender diversity and commitment to creating 'mirrors and windows' for young learners illustrates how authenticity is a method as much as a value.

Similarly, Helen Bushell-Thornalley explores what it means to be openly LGBTQ+ in physical education, sport and dance. Her chapter challenges readers to understand authenticity not only as honest presentation but also as a political stance, requiring both courage and critical awareness. Helen reflects how her own lived experience as an LGBTQ+ educator in Physical Education helps to disrupt norms and open space for new narratives of embodiment and belonging.

All these authors demonstrate that authenticity in education leadership is never static. Rather, as several contributors show, it is an evolving practice that is constantly in flux as it adapts and shifts in response to the context in which it is situated. LGBTQ+ leaders make decisions about what to reveal and when, based on their safety, roles and responsibilities. These are not acts of evasion but of careful calibration. For many of our authors, especially those with intersecting marginalised identities, authenticity is shown to be a vehicle for strategic resistance.

NETWORKS AND COMMUNITY AS DISTRIBUTED AND HORIZONTAL LEADERSHIP

Jo Brassington's exploration of LGBTQ+ networks in education offers a compelling framework for understanding leadership as a collective process. Their co-founding of *Pride & Progress* exemplifies how LGBTQ+ education communities can offer visibility, support and growth for those who might otherwise feel isolated. Brassington's conceptualisation of LGBTQ+ networks as spaces for individual development, group cohesion, and organisational transformation resonates across the book.

Catherine Lee and Dan Buman further this idea by demonstrating how LGBTQ+ leadership development programmes can create spaces for reflection, solidarity, and growth. Their work in structuring and evaluating a leadership development initiative shows how intentionally designed spaces for LGBTQ+ educators provide much more than affirmation. Drawing on Lee's (2020) work, the lived experience of LGBTQ+ educators is shaped by navigating marginalisation, cultivating resilience and fostering empathy. This lived experience positions them uniquely to become excellent leaders who are attuned to inclusion, relational ethics and transformative change. Distinct LGBTQ+ development programmes are then spaces for growth and professional progression but also vehicles for transformative agency in response to adversity.

Charlotte Feather, Catherine Millan and Alex Baird each reflect on how community and mentoring structures enable LGBTQ+ educators to imagine themselves as leaders. Charlotte focuses on the early career phase, where identity and professionalisation often intersect in difficult ways. Catherine highlights how leadership within community contexts and educational institutions is shaped through long-term relationships and presence rather than positional power. Alex demonstrates how the alignment of LGBTQ+ inclusion with academic practice enables educators to leverage their lived experience to challenge normative structures and drive pedagogical and institutional change from within their organisations. Together, these chapters underline the significance of lateral and relational leadership, particularly in institutions that do not always recognise queer forms of influence.

CHALLENGING DOMINANT LEADERSHIP NORMS

The Western depiction of leadership as being embodied by the white, cis, heterosexual man, is dismantled in this book. Contributors challenge the enduring tropes that root educational leadership in hierarchy, individual strength and masculinity. Pippa Sterk demolishes the 'pale, male and stale' leadership model, exposing how entrenched hierarchies stifle diversity, resist accountability and sustain institutional complacency. Pippa extends this critique by interrogating what it means to lead within education systems that require, negotiation, compromise and compliance. They push readers to reflect not only on what leaders do but what they perpetuate, arguing that reflexivity is central to a queer approach to leadership alert to context, history and the distribution of power.

Gary Pykitt's work on inclusive governance offers a sharp critique of top-down models of leadership and instead argues for distributed, participatory and critically conscious structures. His emphasis on accountability reframes leadership as a shared responsibility, embedded in institutional design rather than the authority of isolated individuals. Contributors also draw attention to the emotional and relational dimensions of leadership. Gerlinde Achenbach writes about 'quiet activism' as a form of leadership that is overlooked because it does not conform to more typical performative or hierarchical models. Her work in inclusive policy development, staff training and sustained cultural change exemplifies leadership as care and commitment, rather than power and charisma.

INTERSECTIONALITY AS ETHIC AND METHOD

Intersectionality is not merely referenced in these chapters, it is enacted. Simon Liu demonstrates how effective leadership depends on an understanding of power, privilege and institutional structure. His work in higher education reveals the importance of both data and dialogue in shifting organisational culture. Intersectionality, in this case, is not abstract theory but an operational framework for LGBTQ+ leaders.

Jonny Tridgell reflects on his experience in further education, showing how generational divides, class and race intersect with sexuality to shape his own leadership experience. His candour about the complexity of being 'the only out one' speaks to the complex emotional labour that often accompanies representation. Jonny also illustrates how the responsibility of being 'a role model' can burden and isolate as much as it inspires, especially when structural support is absent elsewhere in education institutions.

Simon and Jonny both demonstrate that leadership through an intersectional lens requires institutions to value complexity rather than flatten it. They advocate for leadership pathways that do not expect assimilation but allow for difference, dissent and innovation. Chapters elsewhere in the book by Richard McDonald, Catherine Lee and Dan Burman in common with Simon and Jonny note that intersectionality deepens not only leadership awareness but pedagogical practice too. Intersectionality in leadership also shapes how leaders relate to students, staff and the wider community.

LEADERSHIP ACROSS THE EDUCATIONAL ECOSYSTEM

One of the book's most significant contributions is its coverage of the full educational landscape. It affirms that leadership is not confined to senior roles or to particular institutions. It is located in nurseries, classrooms, training rooms, university departments and community spaces. LGBTQ+ leadership is enacted through policies and guidance but also through activism, challenge and symbols of LGBTQ+ identities such as pronouns, books and badges. The strength of this collection is that every chapter insists that leadership happens everywhere.

Early years educators such as Kelsey-Ann Caldow and Gerlinde Achenbach foreground the importance of representation and inclusion at the start of educational journeys. Their work shows how early interventions shape not only how the youngest children understand the world but how they understand themselves. Similarly, contributors working in primary and secondary schools, including Holly Coull, George White, Richard McDonald and Jonny Tridgell, show that adolescence is a critical moment for embedding inclusive values and the importance of belonging. What each author conveys, however is the extent to which attempts to promote inclusion and belonging often meet with cultural, religious and political resistance in schools and further education settings.

In higher education, the work of Alex Baird, Charlotte Feather, Catherine Millan, Simon Liu, Pippa Sterk and Helen Bushell-Thornalley illuminates how academic leadership is shaped by competing pressures: research outputs, teaching excellence, compliance and cultural change. Yet their chapters show that LGBTQ+ educators persist in pushing boundaries. They harness teaching, mentoring, training, research and knowledge exchange for inclusive leadership across disciplines. In every case, LGBTQ+ leadership is viewed as something that is lived, shared and constructed in relationship with others.

LEADERSHIP IN AN AGE OF POLITICAL RETREAT

The contributors to this volume write against a backdrop of growing hostility towards LGBTQ+ inclusion. The rollback of rights in the United Kingdom and the United States, the undermining of trans equality, and the erosion of DEI infrastructures are not abstract concerns. They shape the daily reality of educational leaders. Several authors express concern about the chilling effect of new policy and media discourse and its role in the increase in transphobia, discrimination and bullying in education spaces.

And yet, the tone of this book remains one of radical hope. Not optimism in the sense of naïve assurance, but hope in the Freirean (1994) sense, as a form of resistance grounded in action. LGBTQ+ leadership, here, is imagined as a means of survival and transformation. Whether through newsletters, policies, protests or quiet conversations, these educators persist in challenging the status quo. Their work signals that LGBTQ+ leadership is not an afterthought or a woke fad. It is foundational to a humane, responsive and socially just education system.

CALL FOR INVESTMENT AND STRUCTURAL CHANGE: TOWARDS A SUSTAINABLE FUTURE FOR LGBTQ+ LEADERSHIP IN EDUCATION

What this volume demonstrates unequivocally is that we are not facing a shortage of leaders within LGBTQ+ communities. On the contrary, this book is full of examples of bold, values-led, and socially engaged leadership being exercised across every level of the UK education system. What is lacking then is not talent, vision or capacity, but rather the national and institutional commitment and investment required to develop and sustain diverse leadership.

The testimonies gathered in this book illustrate that LGBTQ+ leadership emerges not only through formal hierarchies but also through everyday actions, collective organising and the quiet, radical work of cultural transformation. This leadership is often undertaken with little formal recognition and even less structural support. It is emotional and intellectual labour performed bravely in spaces where policies may be ambiguous, cultures risk-averse and representation scarce. The result is a deeply uneven landscape in which LGBTQ+ leaders frequently assume additional responsibilities, such as mentoring others, driving inclusion work or educating colleagues, usually without the commensurate reward, resourcing or institutional recognition.

To address this imbalance, there is an urgent need for targeted, sustained investment in diverse leadership development. We must support funded research that centres LGBTQ+ leadership as a field of inquiry in its own right. We need robust, intersectional and context-specific studies that inform policy, pedagogy and practice across all educational sectors. Without a solid research base, the contributions of LGBTQ+ leaders remain anecdotal rather than evidentiary, limiting their potential to influence systemic change.

Dedicated LGBTQ+ leadership development programmes have shown time and again that they are transformational for those who take part. These programmes provide safe, reflective spaces where participants can connect personal narratives to leadership practice. They foster skills, confidence and strategic insight while also recognising the distinct challenges of leading from a marginalised position. Programmes such as those described by Lee and Burman in this volume provide a compelling blueprint for what is possible.

Let us then lobby education policy makers to ensure that such programmes are properly funded and resourced.

Education institutions must embed mentoring and sponsorship frameworks that reflect the realities of LGBTQ+ leadership. Traditional models of mentorship often assume shared lived experience or institutional alignment where there is none. Aspirant LGBTQ+ leaders frequently find themselves without senior figures or role models who share or understand their positionality. Mentorship structures must therefore be intentionally designed to support identity-affirming leadership and to counteract the isolation that many contributors in this volume describe. Leadership education itself must also evolve. Courses, qualifications, and training pathways need to engage critically with queer theory, intersectionality, and the lived experiences of LGBTQ+ professionals. These are not supplementary additions to a curriculum; they are essential to the development of inclusive, socially literate leaders. Contributors across the volume challenge time and again the narrow definitions of leadership that dominate current education discourse. Diverse voices and experiences must be reflected in the way we teach, theorise, and assess leadership potential. Finally, we need institutional policies that move beyond performative commitments. Too often, LGBTQ+ inclusion is framed as an issue of compliance, public image or minimal harm reduction. True inclusion demands structural transformation and is embedded in recruitment processes, progression frameworks, governance structures, and cultural norms.

These recommendations are not proposals for charity or symbolic gestures. They are matters of strategic necessity. If educational institutions are to thrive in an increasingly diverse, complex, and contested social landscape, they must recognise LGBTQ+ leadership as an important resource and demonstrate a commitment to aspiring LGBTQ+ leaders. Therefore, to conclude, we offer a message to all those out there who can enact positive change:

To those shaping the future of education: understand that LGBTQ+ educators are not simply adapting to existing leadership paradigms. We are actively innovating and reimagining them. Recognise and celebrate us.

To research funders and policymakers: LGBTQ+ leadership development is not niche work. It is rigorous, urgent and systemically relevant. Please invest time and resource in it.

To those already leading: your voice and visibility are powerful tools for change. You embody the LGBTQ+ leadership that this sector needs.

To those just beginning: you are not alone. You are part of a growing movement of LGBTQ+ educators who lead with integrity, creativity and care.

REFERENCES

Freire, P. (1994). *Pedagogy of hope: Reliving pedagogy of the oppressed*. Bloomsbury.

Lee, C. (2020). Why LGBT teachers may make exceptional school leaders. *Frontiers in Sociology*, 5, 50. https://doi.org/10.3389/fsoc.2020.00050

www.ingramcontent.com/pod-product-compliance
Lightning Source LLC
Chambersburg PA
CBHW061937220426
43662CB00012B/1937